Old Town Houston

Copyright © 2010 Eric DeBeer

All rights reserved. No part of this publication may be reproduced in any form, except for brief quotations in reviews, without written permission from the publisher.

Published in the United States by Eric DeBeer, Houston, Texas.

ISBN 978-0-615-38400-9

Special thanks to

Pepe Reyes

and

Shane Patrick Boyle.

Cover photo: Circa 1910 postcard of Main Street at Preston. Published by Valentine and Sons.

www.oldtownhouston.com

www.oldtownhouston.com

Table of Contents

Map	6
Introduction	11
108 Main Street	12
110 Main Street	18
301 Main	21
304 Main	26
306 Main	29
308 Main	33
310 Main	39
314-320 Main	47
502-504 Main	75
110-112 Travis	80
202 Travis	82
214-218 Travis	84
305-307 Travis	92
309 Travis	98
311 Travis	101
313-317 Travis	110
417-419 Travis	113
910 Prairie	120
912 Prairie	122
914 Prairie	128
813 Congress	130
1016 Congress	140
1402 Congress	147
1417-1419 Congress	153
2215 Congress	155
1200 Rothwell	157
2403 Milam	158
500 Clay	160
1117 Texas	161
1618 Texas	162

MAP #1

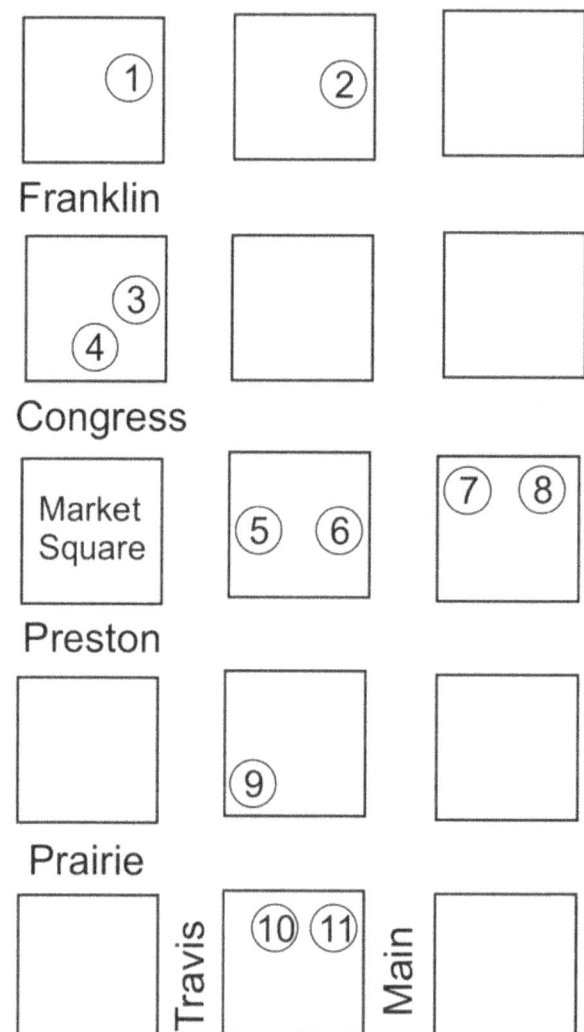

MAP #1

1) 110-112 Travis
2) 108 Main Street and 110 Main Street
3) 202 Travis and 214-218 Travis
4) 813 Congress
5) 305-307 Travis, 309 Travis, 311 Travis, and 313-317 Travis
6) 304 Main, 306 Main, 308 Main, 310 Main, and 314-320 Main
7) 301 Main
8) 1016 Congress
9) 417-419 Travis
10) 910 Prairie, 912 Prairie, 914 Prairie
11) 502-504 Main

Map #2

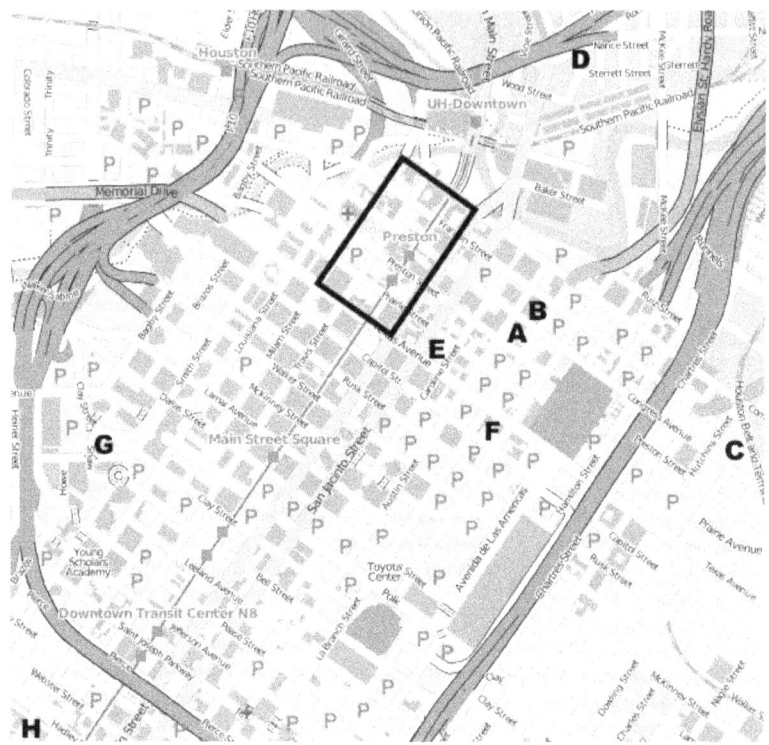

© OpenStreetMap contributors, CC-BY-SA

Map # 2

A) 1402 Congress (intersection of Congress and Austin St.)

B) 1417-1419 Congress (intersection of Congress and La Branch)

C) 2215 Congress (intersection of Congress and Bastrop)

D) 1200 Rothwell (intersection of Rothwell and Walnut)

E) 1117 Texas (intersection of Texas and San Jacinto)

F) 1618 Texas (intersection of Texas and Crawford St.)

G) 500 Clay (intersection of Clay and Shaw)

H) 2403 Milam

Note: The section of the map outlined in a bold black line is detailed on Map #1.

Introduction

Old buildings are works of art that were created layer by layer. They have deeply beautiful patinas that only the passage of time can create. Old buildings give us a real connection with the people of the past. They also continue to shelter us as we create new history.

Houston is a relatively young city, founded in 1836, with a rich history, and a few of these old buildings. Yes, Houston is often criticized for tearing its past down, and it has torn down quite a number of old buildings in the name of progress. But, a few survive and are more appreciated today.

This book focuses on the history of the last surviving nineteenth century commercial and public buildings in Houston. These building were born with great hope and grand openings. Later they were on the brink, left in states of disrepair and abandoned. Today the remaining old buildings of this city have seen resurgence. Many have been restored and have new lives. These building are survivors, which outlasted the rest. The stories of the occupants can be told today within the same walls that existed over one hundred years ago. These people lived their lives here in these Houston buildings, and through these buildings we have a link to their lives.

Each chapter is devoted to a single or related group of addresses. A short history is presented, along with a list of some of the businesses that occupied the building in selected years. Original historical information such as newspaper clippings and biographical essays are also included in select chapters.

I hope you enjoy this short tour through Old Town Houston.

108 Main Street
Brewster Building

The Brewster Building was built on property leased from Robert Brewster sometime between 1872 and 1876. Robert Brewster was in the mercantile business and was an enthusiastic Mason.

This building was the location of Cumming and Sons, Printers. They printed "The Industrial Advantages of Houston, Texas and Environs", an 1894 directory of Houston businesses. This directory was a valuable resource for this book and many of the extended excerpts come from this directory.

The following is a list of some of the businesses that have been located at this address over the years.

Year	Business Name
1894/1895	Cumming & Sons Printers
1897	Lewis Bros & Co
1911/1912	Dorsey Printing Co
1919	Tipps G W Harness
1922	Tipps GW Harness
1934	Army Goods Trading Co
1946	Army Goods Trading Co general merchandise
1955	Army Goods Trading Co general merchandise
1967	Army Goods Trading Co general merchandise
1972	Vacant
1984	Landmark Building

108 Main

108 Main

108 Main

> We keep in stock Elgin butter, Blue Star butter and all grades of Kansas creamery, at the lowest prices; also headquarters for full cream cheese, eggs and poultry.
>
> **LEWIS BROS. & CO.,**
> 108 Main Street, Houston.

Houston Daily Post, December 13, 1897

Robert Brewster [1]

ROBERT BREWSTER was born at Glen Hall, nine miles from Giant's Coffin, in the picturesque county of Derry, north Ireland, on the 7th of March 1812. He is not of Irish blood, however. His parents, Joseph and Nancy Weir Brewster, were both natives of Glasgow, Scotland, the father coming of a long line of Scotch ancestors, and the mother being of Welsh extraction. Robert Brewster was reared in the city of Glasgow, in the schools of which city he received his education. His father was a farmer by occupation, but the sons, four in number, either by chance or from natural inclination, all entered mercantile pursuits, Robert learning the business of linen merchant, which he followed in youth and early manhood in Scotland, north Ireland and England as an itinerant.

In 1840, his father having died and his widowed mother and two brothers and a younger sister having emigrated to America, he decided to come to this country also, and sailed in March of that year from Liverpool, England, by the packet ship Sheridan, of the Black Ball line, reaching New York twenty-eight days later. The spring and summer of that year were spent by him with his people in New York. An older brother, Andrew, who had been in the mercantile business for three or four years at New Orleans, had but a short time previously settled in Houston, and, learning of this, Robert came to Texas in November (1840), and took up his residence in this city. Being still single and in sympathy with the adventurous spirit of the times, he was easily interested in the Santa Fe expedition, which was set on foot the following spring, and but for the timely interference of his brother Andrew he would have joined the

---

[1] From *History Of Texas, Together With A Biographical History Of Tarrant And Parker Counties Containing A Concise History Of The State, With Portraits And Biographies Of Prominent Citizens Of The Above Named Counties, And Personal Histories Of Many Of The Early Settlers And Leading Families.* (1895).

expedition and would of course have shared the fate of its members. Embarking in the mercantile business in Houston in 1841, he was so engaged for about seven years. In the meantime, having decided to make this his home, he married July 8, 1846, taking for a companion Miss Mary C. Andros, then a resident of Houston, but a native of Niagara Falls, New York.

In 1858 Mr. Brewster became Assessor and Collector of Texas for the city of Houston and held this office until the opening of the civil war. He then gave it up, and, not having any particular fondness for public position, has not held any other since, except that of Alderman of the city. He is a Democrat in politics, and, beginning with Lewis Cass in 1848, has voted for the regular Democratic nominee in every presidential election since, as well as for the nominees of his party in all State elections.

In 1844 Mr. Brewster was made a mason, joining Holland Lodge, No. 1, at Houston. He is also a member of Washington Chapter, No. 2, Ruthven Commandery, No. 2, and San Jacinto Lodge of Perfection. He is an enthusiastic Mason, having taken all the degrees in the Ancient York rite up to and including that of Knight Templar, and also those in the Scottish rite up to and including the thirty-second. He became Secretary of the Grand Royal Arch Chapter in 1863, at which time he was also made Grand Recorder of the Grand Commandery of the State, both of which positions he held continuously up to January 1, 1894. At that date he was relieved of the former office, but is still Grand Recorder of the Grand Commandery. He has attended the triennial conclaves of the Grand Commandery of the United States for twenty-odd years, and has a personal acquaintance with many of the most eminent members of this ancient and honored craft.

With his faithful companion, who is still spared to him, Mr. Brewster resides in his large and elegant home, on the corner of Milam Street and Walker Avenue, where the house, the grounds and all of the appointments are suggestive of the well-ordered lives, the intelligence, good taste and generous hospitality of the occupants. Mr. and Mrs. Brewster have had six children, four of whom died in infancy or early childhood. They have a daughter, Mrs. Jane Hart, living in Galveston, and a son, Rev. Mathew D. Brewster, an Episcopal minister, residing in New Orleans, where he holds a charge in his church. Mr. Brewster has but few other near relatives. His mother died at the residence of her son in New York city, New York, in 1865; his eldest brother, Andrew, died in Houston in 1841; his second brother, Joseph, still lives in New York, where he settled in 1835; Sarah, his eldest sister, died in Philadelphia, in 1840, the wife of Hugh McIntyre; Elizabeth died in New York, in 1841; Abram also died in New York, where he had settled many years ago, and Jane died unmarried, in the same State, in 1880. All of the family was communicants of the Episcopal Church.

Now, in his eighty-second year, Mr. Brewster presents the appearance of a man whose life has been well ordered. His temperate and moral habits are unexceptionable. He never indulged in the ruinous pastimes of youth, and, hence, has reached and enjoyed manhood in health, superadded to a sound and practical mind. In disposition he is genial and lively, sanguine in temperament and full of pleasantry; as the old Roman wrote, "a man, and as such interested in all things that concern his kind."

110 Main

This building is often mistakenly referred to as the Raphael building. The mistake can be traced to confusion with the street number changes in the nineteenth century. More research is needed to determine the actual early history of this building.

The following is a list of some of the businesses that have been located at this address over the years.

Year	Business Name
1898	M Allen Wholesale Produce
1911/1912	Girten-Russ Supply Co.
1919	Oil Well Supply
1922	Oil Well Supply Co P&M Oil Co
1934	Produce Café
1946	Travelers Bar Beer
1955	Mike's Traveler's Lounge Beer
1967	Tony's Place Beer
1972	Houlihan's Beer
1976	Saratoga Bar Beer
1984	The Beer Cellar

110 Main

110 Main

110 Main

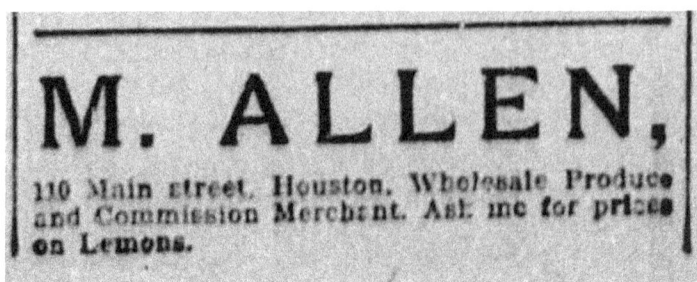

Houston Daily Post, May 1, 1898

301 Main Street Sweeney Coombs & Fredericks Building

The Sweeney Coombs and Fredericks Building was built in 1889. Evidence suggests it was actually a renovation of an earlier structure built in 1861. John Jasper Sweeney, Edward L. Coombs, and Gus Fredericks operated a jewelry store at this site from 1889 to 1907.

The following is a list of some of the businesses that have been located at this address over the years.

Year	Business Name
1895	Sweeney Coombs & Fredericks
1908/1909	Merchants National Bank
1911/1912	Mistrot-Munn Co. Men's Furnishings
1919	United Cigar Stores Co.
1922	United Cigar Stores
1934	United Cigar Stores Co
1946	Rettig's Heap-O-Cream No 8
1955	Burgheim's Pharmacy
1967	Burgheim's Pharmacy
1972	Burgheim's Pharmacy
1976	Dippy's Cafeteria
1984	Harris County Eng Dept (Building Permit Section)

301 Main

301 Main

301 Main

An early view of 301 Main, 1894

Main Street North from Preston - 1915. The Sweeney Combs and Fredericks Building can be seen near the center of the photo.

SWEENEY, COOMBS & FREDERICKS
Jewelers. 301 Main Street [2]

With the advancement of any community, in wealth, intelligence and culture, the fine arts of decoration and adornment prosper and the skill and taste of the jeweler and silversmith are brought more constantly and generally into requisition. Of course those long engaged in the business have done no little to educate and direct the public taste; a work which probably no house in Houston has accomplished more effectually than that of Messrs. Sweeney, Coombs & Fredericks, whose establishment was instituted as Sweeney & Coombs, January 24th, 1874, the present firm being constituted in 1889. The premises occupied consist of a handsome store 100x25 feet in dimensions and the stock, valuing many thousands of dollars, contains an assortment which for beauty and artistic elegance cannot be surpassed in the state. It includes special lines of ladies' jewelry in sets, diamonds, and other precious stones in large variety, plain and ornate rings, French bronzes, marble and ormolu clocks, ceramic and bronze ware, artistic china and bric-a-brac, watches of all the reliable makes, silverware, pitchers, services, card baskets, and tableware, and in short an endless and recherche assortment of those choice and artistic goods which belong only to the highest class in the trade. The house makes direct importations of diamonds and foreign goods, and having the most intimate connections with manufacturers in this country they are enabled to offer the most desirable goods to the public at lowest prices. A special department of the business is fine watch and jewelry repairing and diamond setting. The most expensive and complicated timepiece may be entrusted to the care of this house, with the assurance that it will be skillfully treated and restored in perfect order. Articles of jewelry are made according to

---

[2] From *The Industrial Advantages Of Houston, Texas, And Environs, Also A Series Of Comprehensive Sketches Of The City's Representative Business Enterprises.* (1894).

individual design if required, or manufactured from pattern and design furnished by the firm. The individual members of the firm are Messrs. J. J. Sweeney, E. L. Coombs and Gus Fredericks; all of whom are well known residents, bound up and identified with the advancement and progress of the city. Messrs. Sweeney and Coombs are the owners of the opera house, an illustration of which appears elsewhere in this volume. These gentlemen are among the largest real estate owners in Houston, and they are also identified with other interests of importance. Mr. E. L. Coombs is a director of the Planters and Mechanics Rank, and also of the American Brewing Association. Closing this sketch it is but right to say that the house of Sweeney, Coombs & Fredericks is one of the most popular resorts in South Texas for those in search of genuine values in diamonds, jewelry and silverware-a question which is never in dispute on entering into business relations with this house.

304 Main Street
Stuart Building

The Stuart Building was built between 1879 and 1880. One of four buildings built at the same time: 304, 306, 308, and 310 Main Street. All are called the Stuart Building.

The following is a list of some of the businesses that have been located at this address over the years.

Year	Business Name
1894/1895	Krupp & Tuffly Boots & Shoes/ Pastoriza, J.J. Printers and Stationers
1911/1912	Wolf Shoe Co.
1919	Becker Loan Co / Becker Harris Jeweler
1922	Becker H & Sons Jewelers / Becker Sw & Co Loan
1934	The Rathskeller Beer
1946	Askins Credit Clothing
1955	Askin's Credit Clothing Co.
1967	Reiner's Jewelers
1972	Reiner's Jewelers
1976	Vacant
1984	Eve Fun Shop Gift Shop

304 Main

304 Main

304 Main

Houston Daily Post, July 17, 1897. "Five Room cottage, in Third ward; modern improvements; recently repapered and painted, contains both, hall and two galleries, two cisterns, outhouses, complete; only $15 per month.

306 Main Street
Stuart Building

This building was built between 1879 and 1880. This was the site of Wilkins & Adey Booksellers & Stationers.

The following is a list of some of the businesses that have been located at this address over the years.

Year	Business Name
1880/1881	Lathrop & Wilkins Booksellers and Stationers
1882/1883	Wilkins & Adey Booksellers & Stationers
1896	A.E. Kiesling Druggist
1911/1912	Cawthon K H Banker Broker and Jeweler
1919	Lewis Oyster Parlor
1922	Lewis Fish & Oyster Parlor
1934	Lone Star Bldg & Loan Assn
1946	Merchants & Employees Industrial Bank Loans
1955	Merchants & Employees Industrial Bank
1972	Cinema X Inc Theatre
1984	Cinema X Inc Theatre

306 Main

306 Main

306 Main

K.H. Cawthon Banker, Pawnbroker, & Jeweler, Circa 1911

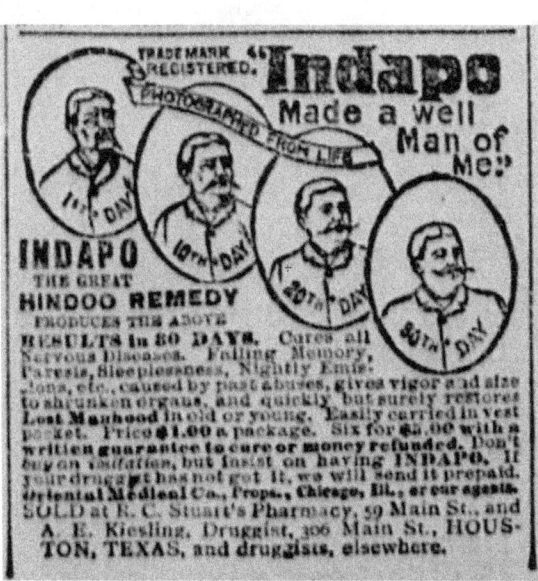

A. E. Kiesling druggist ad, Houston Daily Post, March 16, 1896

306 Main

THE WAR IN AFRICA

Will no doubt render the scarcity of desirable goods more serious and still further increase the prices. We are sure prices will not be lower. Nothing can be gained and much be lost by delaying purchases for HOLIDAY PRESENTS. We have on hand an ENORMOUS STOCK of FINE DIAMONDS in RINGS, PINS, BROOCHES, STUDS, Etc.

SPECIAL OFFER FOR XMAS PRESENTS.

DIAMONDS.

1 Solitaire Diamond Rings, each	$20.00
2 Solitaire Diamond Rings, each	30.00
4 Solitaire Diamond Rings, each	45.00
2 Solitaire Diamond Rings, each	60.00
1 Solitaire Diamond Ring	125.00
2 Solitaire Diamond Rings, each	200.00
5 Solitaire Diamond Rings, each	25.00
3 Solitaire Diamond Rings, each	50.00
6 Solitaire Diamond Rings, each	70.00
5 Solitaire Diamond Rings, each	150.00
2 Solitaire Diamond Rings, each	225.00
1 Solitaire Diamond Ring	300.00
Diamond Pins, Studs, Earrings, Brooches and Charms, $10 to	125.00

Your choice of new mountings with no extra price.

WATCHES.

Gents' fine 14-kt. Gold Case, 17 jewels, your choice of movement	$35.00
Gents' fine 14-kt. Gold Case, 15 jewels, your choice of movement	25.00
Railroad Watch, 17 jewels, Hampden, Elgin or Waltham, nickel case	12.50
B. W. Raymond, 17 jewels, nickel case	12.50
B. W. Raymond, 15 jewels, nickel case	10.00
Appleton & Tracy, 17 jewels, 20-year case	15.00
Elgin, 23 jewels, 20-year case	22.50
Hampden, 21 jewels, 20-year case	25.00
Ladies', 14-kt. case, Elgin or Waltham movement, $17.50, $20,	25.00
Ladies', 14-kt. case, Elgin movement, diamond set, $25, $40,	85.00
Ladies', 14-kt. filled case, Elgin movement, $10, $15,	20.00

We have all makes of Watches, in price from $10 to $250.

In making the above prices we want you to bear in mind that while these goods are comparatively new and we guarantee them in every particular, they are unredeemed pledges and the above prices only represent one-third or one-fourth of their real value. Make your selection now before the holiday rush sets in, and if desired they can be delivered at a later date.

Sweeney Loan Office
306 Main Street

Money to Loan on Anything of Value. Money Loaned on Bonds, Stocks and all kinds of Collateral.

Houston Daily Post, November 19, 1899

308 Main Street
Stuart Building

This building is also part of the Stuart Buildings built between 1879 and 1880. This was the site of James F Dumble purveyor china, glassware, queensware, crockery, and house furnishing goods. Another important early tenant was Sakowitz Bros. Clothiers, they would later move into the Kiam Building.

The following is a list of some of the businesses that have been located at this address over the years.

Year	Business Name
1880/1881	Dumble James F China Glassware and Queensware crockery and house furnishing goods
1899	Lipper The Hatter
1911/1912	Sakowitz Bro's Clothiers
1919	Dover S P Men's Furnishings
1922	Dover S P Clothing
1934	Wilson-Baxter Clothiers
1946	Halls Style Shop Clothiers
1955	Hall's Credit Co
1967	Yale's Credit Clothiers
1972	Yale's Credit Clothiers
1976	Vacant
1984	Jolar Cinema Adult Movie

308 Main

308 Main

SAKOWITZ BROTHERS

THE GOOD
Clothes and Hat Shop
FOR MEN

308 Main Street

The Jewish Herald, early 20th century

308 Main

Houston Daily Post, March 13, 1898

Houston Daily Post, October 10, 1896

SIMON SAKOWITZ[3]

As an illustration of what straightforwardness, integrity and an intelligent application to one's work may accomplish, the career of Mr. Simon Sakowitz of Houston, Texas, is eminently worth while perusing and contemplating.

Mr. Sakowitz is a young man who has carved his own career, yet he is today among the most highly esteemed residents and business men of the progressive and flourishing city of Houston, Texas. He was born on January 1, 1884, in Kiev, Russia, the son of Louis and Lina Sakowitz, and arrived in this country in 1890. His family settled in Galveston, Texas, where Simon attended public school for a period of only one year, and then, at the age of ten, he started to work as errand boy in a store. Step by step he worked his way up, at first becoming salesman and then manager of that store. After he and his brother Tobias had saved up about twelve hundred dollars, they determined to establish a business of their own, and in 1903 they organized the firm of Sakowitz Brothers. This business, under their able managership, grew and developed to such an extent that, after six years, they decided to branch out further, and so they bought out a concern in Houston, Texas, and Simon Sakowitz removed to that city and assumed the managership of the new business.

The full measure of success with which the ability of Mr. Sakowitz has been rewarded may be seen from the fact that the firm of Sakowitz Brothers, at Main and Preston streets in Houston, is today counted among the biggest concerns that deal in men's, boys' and children's clothing.

The most beautiful part of Mr. Sakowitz's career, however, is that hard work and his own remarkable success has not made him indifferent to the struggles and sufferings

---

[3] From *Eminent Jews Of America: A Collection Of Biographical Sketches Of Jews Who Have Distinguished Themselves In Commercial, Professional And Religious Endeavor.* (1918).

of his fellow men. For he is a liberal contributor to all the Jewish charities and institutions of Houston and takes a deep interest in every movement of an altruistic and ameliorative character.

In August 1909, Mr. Sakowitz was married to Miss Clara B. Bowsky of New Orleans, and they are now the happy parents of two fine children, Julia N. and Louise.

310 Main Street
Stuart Building

This building is the last part of the Stuart Buildings built between 1879 and 1880. This was the site of an important dealer of sheet music and musical instruments, Clifford Grunewald.

The following is a list of some of the businesses that have been located at this address over the years.

Year	Business Name
1894/1895	Grunewald, Clifford Music
1899	C. Gruenwald Music and Musical Instruments
1911/1912	Sweeney Loan Co.
1919	Mistrot G A & Co Ladies Ready To Wear
1922	Levy Lm Ladies Ready To Wear
1934	Day's Clothiers
1946	Day's Credit Clothiers
1955	Day's Credit Clothiers
1967	Day's Department Store
1972	Day's Dept Store
1976	Day's Dept Store
1984	S&S Sandwich Shop

310 Main

310 Main

310 Main

Sidewalk entrance to Days Department Store.

Sweeney Loan Company, circa 1911

310 Main

Clifford Grunewald

"Home Influences That Elevate. Are those where music permeates every nook and corner of your domicille, as often as your leisure hours will permit. Love and music should make home a heaven. A mandolin, guitar, violin or banjo with accompaniment of a Knabe or Fisher piano, should draw the family toward the hearth stone with the same power that Orpheus charmed Eurydice from Hades." Houston Daily Post, February 2, 1898.

"Men Are Deceptive sometimes, and so are pianos. A handsome outside is no promise of the merit within. So in choosing a piano exercise the same care as you would in choosing a husband. Get a Knabe or Fischer piano and you will get one with more real music to the square inch than in many other pianos. We will sell you one on terms that will please you. Lots of calls for serenade music. I have it." Houston Daily Post, February 5, 1898.

310 Main

"A Pleasure to Children to practice their lessons if they have one of our Patent Adjustable Spring Back Plush Seated Piano Chairs. We now have on exhibition several very handsome late styles of cheap Pianos, which will sell on easy terms." Houston Daily Post, April 30, 1898.

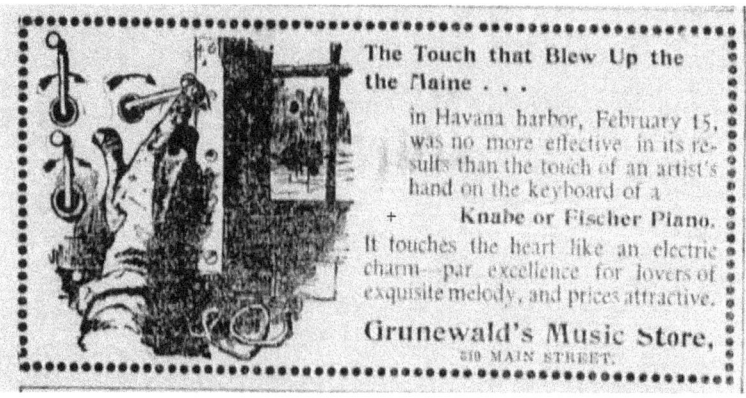

"The Touch that Blew Up the Maine in Havana harbor, February 15, was no more effective in its results than the touch of an artist's hand on the keyboard of a Knabe or Fischer Piano. It touches the heart like an electric charm - par excellence for lovers of exquisite melody, and prices attractive." Houston Daily Post, May 4, 1898.

C. GRUNEWALD,
Dealer in Pianos, Organs, Etc.,
310 Main Street. [4]

The above emporium of music is one of the leading ones of the State and contains a stock of goods worthy the attention of the most fastidious. The business is one of the oldest established in Houston. It dates back to the year 1872, when it was founded by Mr. Renzo Grunewald. In 1879 the proprietorship became vested in the hands of Mr. Louis Grunewald, of New Orleans. In 1880 Mr. Cliff Grunewald became the manager of the business in this city, and in 1882 he became its proprietor. Two years later, at New Orleans, was formed the L. Grunewald Co., Limited, and this organization took stock in the enterprise here, and Mr. Cliff Grunewald was also interested in the general business of the company. Later he bought out their interest in the Houston establishment and has since conducted it entirely on his own account. The house carries a large stock of pianos and organs, the product of some of the leading manufacturers of the country. They are the sole agents here for the Knabe, Fischer and Mehlin pianos and the Mason & Hamlin, Storey & Clark and Dyer & Hughes organs. The above may be said to be renowned for their splendid tone and power, good workmanship and general excellence. The house also carries a complete assortment of classical and popular sheet and book music and musical publications of American, English, French, German and Italian origin, and the facilities of the house are such that the most favorable terms are obtained here. Pianos and organs are sold on the installment plan when required and easy payments give every facility to people of moderate means to obtain these now almost indispensable articles of household comfort and enjoyment. Mr. Cliff Grunewald, the proprietor, enjoys an

---

[4] From *The Industrial Advantages Of Houston, Texas, And Environs, Also A Series Of Comprehensive Sketches Of The City's Representative Business Enterprises.* (1894).

experience of the business extending over nearly his whole life, both in this country and in Europe. He thoroughly understands the public demands and is altogether able to satisfy every legitimate requirement. He is an accomplished pianist and vocalist and a composer of dance music of considerable merit. He is very popular in social and society circles and is a member of the B.P.O. Elks, Knights of Pythias, Turn Verein, German-American Society, Grunewald Quartette, Houston Light Guards, Catholic Knights of America, and is of the choir of the Church of the Annuciation.

314, 316, 318, 320 Main Street
Kiam Building and annex

The Kiam Building was built in 1893 by Ed Kiam for his Kiam's Mammoth Clothiers. Kiam's sold gentleman furnishings and he was a prolific advertiser. This building had the first electric elevator in Houston.

Sakowitz Brothers occupied the building from 1918 to 1928.

Today a portion of the building is occupied by Notsuoh, a popular bar and music venue among the art crowd. Jim Pirtle is the owner of Notsuoh. The name Notsuoh is Houston spelled backwards. Notsuoh was also the name of an early Houston carnival similar to Mardi gras.

314, 316, 318, 320 Main

The following is a list of some of the businesses that have been located at these addresses over the years.

Year	Business Name
314 MAIN, 316 MAIN	
1890'S	Kiam Ed Clothing
1908/1909	Kiam Ed Clothing
1911/1912	Kiam Shoe Co., Kiam Ed Clothing
1919	Sakowitz Bros Clothing, Sakowitz Bros Clothing
1922	Sakowitz Bros Clothing, Sakowitz Bros Clothing
1934	Warren Bros Clothiers
1946	Askins Credit Clothing, Dean's Credit Clothiers
1955	Clark's Credit Clothiers, Dean's Credit Clothiers
1967	Clark's Credit Clothiers, Dean's Credit Clothiers
1972	Clark's Credit Clothiers, Dean's Credit Clothiers
1976	Clark's Credit Clothiers, Dean's Credit Clothiers
1984	Whites Sellis Jewelry & Pawn Shop, Dean's Credit Clothiers
318 MAIN, 320 MAIN	
1893	Ed Kiam Gents Furnishing Goods
1908/1909	Kiam Ed Clothing, Kiam Ed Clothing
1911/1912	Kiam Ed Clothing, Kiam Ed Clothing
1919	Sakowitz Bros Clothing, Sakowitz Bros Clothing
1922	Sakowitz Bros Clothing, Sakowitz Bros Clothing
1934	Byrd's Inc Men's Furnishings
1946	Nelson's Taurpaulin Shop, Economy Shoe Corner
1955	Economy Shoe Corner
1967	Cannon's Economy Shoe Corner
1972	Cannon's Economy Shoe Corner
1976	Cannon's Economy Shoe Corner
1984	Vacant

314, 316, 318, 320 Main

THE NEW KIAM BUILDING.

Houston Daily Post, November 7, 1893

314, 316, 318, 320 Main

314, 316 Main

314, 316, 318, 320 Main

320 Main, Kiam Building

314, 316, 318, 320 Main

Early Photo of The Kiam Building

314, 316, 318, 320 Main

Kiam Building, circa 1911

Houston Daily Post, October 26, 1902

314, 316, 318, 320 Main

Houston Daily Post, January 1, 1894

Entrance to Dean's Credit Clothing, 316 Main

314, 316, 318, 320 Main

Houston Daily Post, March 1, 1896

Houston Daily Post

314, 316, 318, 320 Main

Daper gentlemam from a Kiam's advertisment. Houston Daily Post, June 2, 1901

314, 316, 318, 320 Main

Houston Daily Post, March 29, 1896

314, 316, 318, 320 Main

Edward Kiam

Ed Kiam[5]

A stranger dropping into the city of Houston and strolling along its main thoroughfares in search of whatever there may be of interest to be seen by a casual observer cannot fail to be struck with the really metropolitan appearance of some of the buildings that meet his eye, and the unique and tasteful displays of goods that adorn the show windows of many of the largest emporiums of trade in that city. The establishment of Ed Kiam, at the corner of Main street and Preston avenue, will be sure to attract his attention, and whether he stops to take a survey of the splendid five-story brick building or the handsome exhibit of masculine apparel arranged in 170 feet of show windows fronting on two streets, the conviction will be speedily forced on his mind that behind that vast pile of brick and mortar, frescoing and plate-glass, fabrics, furnishing, tinsel and texture, neatly and artistically arrayed, there must be some enterprise, some money and some business sense. The wonder and admiration of the stranger will be all the more excited, should he, stepping inside and asking to see the proprietor, have pointed out to him a young man but little past thirty years of age.

Ed. Kiam and his mammoth clothing-house are both distinctively Texas products. Mr. Kiam was born in the old town of Liberty, Liberty County, Texas, January 14, 1864, being a son of Victor and Sarah Kiam, who emigrated from Alsace France, about the year 1851, and settled at Liberty. Ed. was reared, however, in Houston, his parents moving to this city in 1866. His father was a former well-known merchant of this place, and died here in 1887. The subject of this brief notice began his business career at the age of fourteen as a clerk in the clothing-store of Joe Mills, in this city, and remained in Mills' employ some four years. At the

---

[5] From *History Of Texas, Together With A Biographical History Of Tarrant And Parker Counties Containing A Concise History Of The State, With Portraits And Biographies Of Prominent Citizens Of The Above Named Counties, And Personal Histories Of Many Of The Early Settlers And Leading Families.* (1895).

314, 316, 318, 320 Main

end of that time he formed a partnership with Levi Sam, and opened a clothing-house in a little frame building on the site of his present establishment. After a partnership of two years with Sam he sold his interest to the latter, and, associating himself with his brother, Ben, he opened a clothing-store at the corner of Main Street and Congress Avenue, under the firm name of Kiam Brothers, which was carried on successfully for three years. He then bought his brother's interest, and shortly afterward, taking a fifty-year lease on a lot, on the corner of Main Street and Preston Avenue, there erected the elegant structure now known as the "Kiam Building," which with the buildings he has adjoining it on the east, gives him a frontage of 100 feet on Main Street and running back 100 feet on Preston Avenue. This structure is built of brick, with stone trimmings, and is equipped with all modern conveniences, being lighted throughout with electricity, furnished with water from the city water works and reached, above the first floor, by an electric-motor elevator. The two lower floors are occupied by Mr. Kiam with his large stock of men's and boy's clothing and furnishing goods, the three upper floors being used as offices. The location of the building, it being central to business and all places of public importance, together with its superior equipments, makes office room in its especially desirable, and insures a good class of tenants.

Mr. Kiam does a very large business, and his success is due to his sound judgment, his tact and his intelligent activity. He is one of the tireless, sleepless and irrepressible advertisers of Houston, and he has demonstrated that it pays to be such

The following letter was submitted as evidence in a civil case in which Ed Kiam was sued by a former employee.

Hickey et al v. Kiam[6]

Ed Kiam, Mammoth Clothier, 314 to 320 Main Street, Cor. Preston Avenue, Houston, Texas. Oct. 2nd, '02. Mrs. Kate Hickey, c/o G. Y. Smith, Fort Worth, Texas — Dear Madam: Referring to your letter of September the 30th, we have an opening in our women's altering department and want a good forewoman. If you think that you are capable of holding a position of this sort, we will start you on a salary of $15.00 per week, and if your services are satisfactory you will have a position with us as long as you wish to keep it. The position is permanent and your chances for advancement are good, as we wish to pay our people well, when they show that they are working to our interest.

We will make an opening for your daughter in our alteration department, and we will pay her a reasonable salary. We do not know what her salary is now, but we will pay her $1.00 more than she is getting where she is at.

We wish you and your daughter to both understand that we are not trying to get you down here just to keep you here until the season is over and then let you both out. We want you to be a fixture with us in this town and you will have a good and satisfactory position with us as long as you wish to keep it.

The ladies' ready-to-wear business we have just gone into, and it is entirely a new business with us. We have been handling heretofore clothing and furnishings for men and boys of this city for the past 25 years, and the women's business we opened on the 22nd of September.

---

[6] From *The Southwestern Reporter.* (1905).

314, 316, 318, 320 Main

We have done a very good business since we opened, and have every reason to believe that the department is going to be a success.

You must understand if you accept this position you will have to come with us at once, as we want someone in the workrooms immediately, and if you know of some other good woman in Fort Worth that is a good fitter you can also bring her with you, and we will start her on $12.00 per week, with a permanent position.

Kindly wire me immediately upon receipt of this letter whether or not you will accept, and if you do accept, state when you can be here and state at the same time if your daughter will be with you, and if you are successful in getting another woman, also mention that fact. Yours very truly, ED. KIAM.

314, 316, 318, 320 Main

ELECTRO-GALVANIC SANITARIUM,
Kiam Building Annex.[7]

The value of electricity as a curative agent for the many ills which human flesh is heir to, is generally understood and conceded by all who have any pretensions to latter day science. But we are of the opinion that to avail ourselves of the benefits that this wonderful fluid offers to mankind, it must be administered intelligently under the auspices and direction of those who make a specialty of this particular line of treatment. In this city at the present time Drs. Mrs. Balfour and C. H. Warner, afford to the public the greatest facilities in this direction. Their Electro-Galvanic Sanitarium in the Kiam building-annex is provided with all conveniences and facilities, which enable them to give to patients a full and proper course of treatment, under the most favorable conditions. Our purpose here is simply confined to pointing out to our readers the fact that such an establishment exists here in the city, and to advise them at the same time to make such inquiries and investigations as will be sure to establish the verity of all that is claimed for and by the institution. The electro-galvanic treatment, when judiciously administered, often succeeds after medicine and all other means have failed, and combined with massage, vapor and medicated baths, its results are often simply marvelous. Surgical operations performed, assisted by the influence of electricity are far more efficacious in certain cases than otherwise, the pain also being considerably lessened. As regards the use of baths, the care of Drs. Balfour & Warner alleviation and cure is effected of a large number of chronic and other diseases, notably throat and lung diseases, blood poisoning, nervous diseases, affections of the kidneys, female diseases, neuralgia, gout, rheumatism, etc. In obesity the best of results are obtained,

---

[7] From *The Industrial Advantages Of Houston, Texas, And Environs, Also A Series Of Comprehensive Sketches Of The City's Representative Business Enterprises.* (1894).

the patient losing flesh without the slightest injury to health. Special treatment for all skin and blood diseases is also given. Balfour's Complexion Bleach has had a great success, and insures a brilliant complexion without injury to the skin. We have not the space to devote further to the subject, but as before said, refer all interested direct to headquarters, where they will meet with all attention and courtesy. The Electro-Galvanic Sanitarium was established in this city January 1, 1884. It occupies nearly an entire floor of the Kiam building annex. The proprietors are Dr. Mrs. Balfour and Dr. C.H. Warner. Dr. Balfour has received her education at some of the finest massage institutions in the country, and she is eminently qualified for her work. Dr. Warner is a graduate of a high-class medical college at Gottingen, Germany, taking his degree there in 1858. He has made a long life study of the special vocation, and among other places he has practiced at Hot Springs, Ark., and for some years had an establishment at Galveston, where they are endorsed by and refer to the leading professional and business residents of that city.

314, 316, 318, 320 Main

THE KIAM BUILDING[8]

WHICH IS THE PRIDE OF ALL HOUSTON.

New and Elegant Home of an Enterprising and Prosperous Merchant.

A TOWERING STRUCTURE OF BRICK AND IRON

With Beautiful and Convenient Store Rooms and Offices-The Formal Opening Which Occurred Yesterday Was One of the Events in the City.

WHICH WILL LONG BE REMEMBERED

As One of the Most Charming and Enjoyable-A History of Mr. Kiam's Business, Showing the Remarkable Development and Progress Made by Him

FROM THE START UP TO THE PRESENT TIME.

A Full Description of This Substantial and Magnificent Building Which is Undoubtedly the Grandest in Houston, and One That Can Be Classed as Ranking Amongst the Model Building of the Large Eastern Cities.

Kiam's opening took place yesterday, and was a success.
Preparations for the event had been in progress for several days, and the result was so greatly in excess of the

---

[8] From The Houston Daily Post. (November 7, 1893).

expectations of Mr. Kiam and his little army of assistants as to prove almost astounding.

The hour designated to begin receiving the public was 4:30 p.m., and as promptly as the clock strikes, twos and threes, then dozens, and a little later hundreds, came, filling the floor space and exchanging complimentary allusions to what they saw. Men, women, and children for four hours came and went in a steady stream, so great that the wide arched doorway was packed and jammed. The utmost of good humor prevailed, or the crushed draperies and creased clothes would not have been viewed so complacently.

The main entrance to the building is on Main Street, close to the corner of Preston Avenue. The open portal, with its broad, tessellated floor, is a welcome to all, and had been supplemented with some of nature's most beautiful things. To the left of the entrance looking inward was a magnificent hibiscus in full bloom, sent with its stand with the compliments of Mrs. Dr. E. P. Davis. To the right was a pineapple all but ready to take on the hue of ripeness, sent with the compliments of Mrs. Westgate. In front of the entrance and a dozen feet away stood a large triple mirror, at it's base a mass of evergreens and flowering plants and above it a horse-shoe of huge dimensions that bore the card of Abe Levy. Above this an exquisite piece, a star in roses of all the colors of the rainbow, was suspended, with the card of the donor, W. L. Foley, nestling in its perfume-laden bed.

These, with the mirror, formed the center of a suspended piece shaped in bay leaves and telling of "Kiam's Opening."

Along the right aisle to the front the eye wandered amid artistically displayed goods intermingled with decorations in evergreen until the dividing line of the lower floor was reached. To the left of this division was another triple mirror, tastefully decorated, at its base a handsome floral cushion sent with the compliments of C. H. Sprong.

This was supported upon the opposite side by a handsome and heavy mass of flowers, the elegant arrangement needing nothing to indicate the handiwork of Mrs. Dr. Rutherford.

The division was marked by an arch in white, with evergreens arranged in the word "Welcome," beneath which was suspended a floral ladder, sent from Galveston with the compliments of E. S. Levy.

From front to rear of the great building extend counters bearing immense loads of clothing, and between the pillars are placed upright showcases, in native wood, containing furnishing goods. Between these counters the white fluted columns show, and each one was twined in ivy that clung so naturally as to seem to have had only nature's training. The same order of decoration made of each of the score of double gas jets a thing of beauty.

At the rear of the store and elevated above any obstruction to the view is the cashier's gallery, utilized yesterday for a band stand. The decorations were in simple green, profusely used and blending well with the brown of the native woods upon which it hung. Herb and Lewis' orchestra had been engaged for the occasion and when the gentlemen and their assistants took their place at 4:40 the store was already full of people. With the entrancing strains of popular air's rendered by this excellent band, the constant passing and repassing of ladies, gentlemen and children and the sound of cheerful voices and merry laughter, the solid place of business was transformed for the time into a hall of pleasure and it required no great stretch of the imagination to conceive that a promenade concert of the first order was in progress in a sylvan bower. The programme for the occasion was as follows, the grand piano being a compliment by Mr. C. Grunewald:

FIRST PART.

1. Kiam's Opening March (specially dedicated to the grand opening by Professors Herb and Lewis.

2. Grand Selection—"Grand Duchess".......Offenbach.
3. Waltz-"Columbian Exposition:...Herrmann.
4. Medley-"The Merry Soubrette"..................................……..De Witt.
5. Quintette-"Love's Dream After the Ball"…………..Zybulka.
6. Grand Selection-"Faust"……………………….......………..Gounod.
7. "My Ideal"-(Characteristic)................................Hermann.

INTERMISSION.

SECOND PART.

8. Overture-"Tone Pictures of the North and South…………...…..Bennedix.
9. Selection-"Isle of Champagne"…………………….............…………Furst.
10. Waltz-"Leona"………………………………............…Stahl.
11. Grand Selection-"Tannhauser"……………………….........…Wagner.
12. Quintette-"Shelm Amor"…………………………….....…...Ellenberg.
13. Selection-"Wang"………………………………...………Morse.
14. Police Patrol……………………………………..........…Stahl.

On the second floor a reception room for the ladies had been prepared, extending from an elegant boudoir-like alcove at the front to the elevator at the rear. Chairs, settees, small tables, pot plants, clinging vines and fragrant flowers combined to make this portion of the building one of its most attractive spots, and it was duly appreciated by ladies who sought for a few moments of rest from the bustle and jam upon the lower floor.

The decorations upon this floor were not so elaborate as upon the floor below, but displayed rather good taste in the arrangement and were greatly admired. All the vantage points were seized upon to sustain and display the trailing vines and bunches of evergreen that took the place of the flowers, which, but for the long drought, might have been found in plenty to render beautiful the whole of the great Kiam establishment.

Not so great a crowd of people has ever been seen in Houston upon a similar occasion-even as Houston has not before seen such an establishment. Like the giant oak that from a tiny shoot that from a little acorn sprung, has in years grown and grown, until it is the admiration of all who behold it, the house of Kiam has grown until there is scarce its like in all this great state.

Scarcely a house in Houston tonight is without the name of Kiam, as handsome souvenirs in the shape of costly pictures, each in its own receptacle, had been provided for the ladies and each lady caller was presented with one of these. Nothing prettier could have been conceived.

The children were not forgotten, either, but each one was presented with a souvenir box containing things that are used in the school work, and of which each urchin and little miss is duly proud.

So much for the inside work, save that the holiday appearance of the interior was augmented by the appearance of each attaché of the establishment in full dress, and that it was subject of general remark that no more suave and polite body of gentlemen could possibly be gathered together than that headed by Ed Kiam.

The view from the outside of the building was charming. The skill of long experience and the taste which is unapproached by art had free ground for its exercise in the great show windows, more than a dozen in number, that may be seen from both Main street and Preston avenue, and they were viewed with pleasure by the thousands who came to the grand opening. Happily blended colors and the tasteful arrangement of the varied classes of goods in which the house deals caught every eye.

At night the building was bright inside as gas and electric light could make it, and from the streets it shone resplendent, every window lighted and the five stories showing clear and well defined. Away high up the window lights shone like stars, and the blaze of light below shown yet upon the moving multitude until long past the hour designated for the close of the reception, Mr. Haas, the manger, estimated that not less than 17,000 people greeted Ed Kiam on his opening day, which was not the least monument to his energy and fine business acumen. The memory of the gala time will be cherished and "the day of Kiam's Opening" will hereafter be a landmark in Houston time.

The new establishment of Mr. Ed Kiam, located on the corner of Main street and Preston avenue, of the principal business corners in the city of Houston, which has been the talk of the town and every visitor in here lately, and that attracted so much attention while in the course of construction has been completed to the letter and turned over to the pushing and wide-awake man whose name it bears, and as said before is the handsomest architectural adornment of Houston. Note this fact that the building was erected during one of the gloomiest financial periods in the history of the country, at a time when others would note dare to embark into a new enterprise and particularly one on such a mammoth scale.

Good judgment, grit and energy will accomplish most anything undertaken in an honest way and Mr. Kiam is fortunate in possessing all these gifts, so pushed to completion as rapidly as possible his present fine store, notwithstanding the dark outlook for a resume of business as it stood less than twelve moths ago.

Workmen were hard at it both day and night and manifested a great interest in the desire of Mr. Kiam to get the last nail driven, the last brick laid, in this business block at an early day, and finally they pulled him through and made him happy.

The building in question has a grand commanding site, and its five stories of brick and iron tower high above all the surroundings with imposing effect.

The building occupies 100x100 feet. It is in the main five stories and the basement in height, with high ceilings, abundance of light and ventilation heated throughout by steam, lighted by gas and electricity and equipped with the modern Hale elevator, (the same style and make as that used in the Manufacturers' building at the Chicago World's Fair), which affords safe and easy access to the upper floors, and is the first passenger elevator ever used in a business house in South Texas. Mr. Kiam occupies the first two floors with his various departments, while the third, fourth and fifth floors are used for offices, which, owing to their superior quality and adaptability for this use are rapidly being filled up by doctors, lawyers, insurance men and others. The basement has a high ceiling, is well lighted.

The first floor is set apart by Mr. Kiam for men's clothing, hat and cap and gent's furnishing departments, all of which are the most complete of any in the South: and of this spacious floor it may be truly said there are non better equipped or more admirably adapted to the purpose anywhere in any city. The immense show windows permit of nearly 200 lineal feet of display, which Mr. Kiam knows so well how to make attractive, his taste in dressing show windows being unsurpassed.

The large open floor space enables the immense stock to be well and attractively displayed, so that customers may be quickly accommodated.

The second floor has received more than ordinary care in arrangement, for if Mr. Kiam excels in any one department over another it is the department of boys' clothing. Here the boys, the future governors and presidents, come to feast their eyes upon the sea of clothing, hats, caps, furnishing, etc., provided to fit them out in the latest styles for the least money. A portion of this spacious floor is also occupied by the departments of men's and boy's overcoat and a packing and shipping room.

There is a good treatment of detail and enrichment about the entrance.

Every convenience has been provided.

Dressing rooms that in their luxuriance resemble the finest Pullman.

Toilet rooms for ladies and gents. Cash carrier service, speaking tubes connecting the office and various departments, commodious business offices, wrapping desk, tailoring department; a reserve stock room which, by the way, resembles a large wholesale establishment from the vast surplus stock that is always kept in reserve to supply the enormous demands for merchandise which this institution is called upon to furnish from all parts of Texas, Eastern Louisiana and Northern Mexico.

The enormous growth of Mr. Kiam's business and the development of his prosperity within the last decade is a fact recognized by all of the citizens of Houston. The magnitude of what he has achieved is readily vividly realized here in our midst when we stop only a moment to think how his business stood only a few short years ago. From the time he commenced business, which was on a very small scale, he has stuck to the Main street block between Preston and Congress Avenue. It will be seen that in the general march to the front by business men of the city and other much large cities than Houston he has not lagged behind, but has kept abreast of them all.

The growth of his business can readily be comprehended by all who remember his place when he first started out to brave the world for himself in a small two story 20x40 foot building and dropped in his grand opening yesterday. Ten years is but a brief span in the life of an enterprising business, but to look back that time will reveal a growth and expansion in his exclusive trade that is phenomenal. The house now is unquestionably the leading clothing and gents' furnishing establishment in the Southwest: he has far outstripped all of the merchants of adjoining cities in his progressive road. He has climbed the ladder of success from the lowest round to the present high position he now occupies in the estimation of all citizens of the city and business men throughout the country.

He surely has the right kind of pluck and push to be successful and is endowed with extraordinary business qualifications as most all agree. His personal magnetism and tact making and retaining friends is wonderful.

His restless spirit never permits him to be satisfied; his desire and aim is always for improvement.

When one looks in amazement at some gigantic enterprise in its completeness how little thought is given to detail, which was necessary to make the whole harmonious. In all great undertakings it is the careful attention to detail, the constant watching of the little things, which are essential to success. In the intricacies of mechanism if the little cogs or parts fail to perform their functions all will go awry. And so it is in business. The systematic methods, the care of little things no matter how apparently trivial in themselves and the blending of detail are all necessary to form the concrete mass which makes the whole perfect and insures success in all undertaking.

Mr. Kiam pays strict attention to every little detail connected with his business; is thoroughly familiar with the wants and demands of the public and his many customers.

The popularity of his establishment is of course due to some extent through the enterprise he shows in ordering goods, which are all in accordance with the latest dictates of fashion.

502, 504 Main Street
Stegeman Building

This building was built by Frederick W. Stegeman around 1879. Stegeman was a partner of Stegeman and Wagner Ornamental Ironworks.

The following is a list of some of the businesses that have been located at these addresses over the years.

Year	Business Name
1880/1881	Mason J.T. Dry Goods
1886/1887	Wright, C.J. Photography
1894/1895	Buckley Bro's Boot and Shoemakers/ Wright C.J. Photographers
1896	A.E. Kiesling Druggist
1911/1912	Walter Frank J Saloon, Kiesling Adolph E Druggist
1919	American Confectionery, Kiesling A E Drugs
1934	Bradley's Women's Clothiers, Ellan's Hat Shop
1946	Ellan's Hat Shop Inc
1967	Houston Costume Co
1972	Houston Costume Co
1976	Vacant

502, 504 Main

Early Photo of The Stegeman Building

502, 504 Main

502, 504 Main

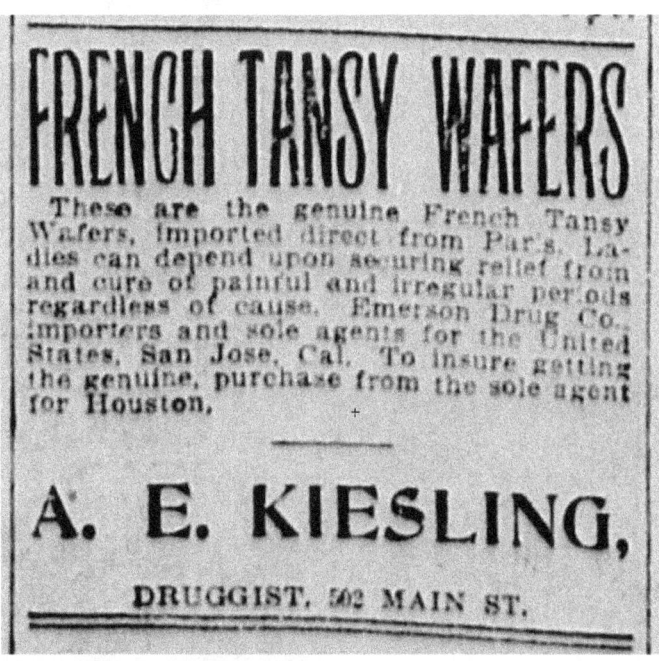

Houston Daily Post, April 13, 1897

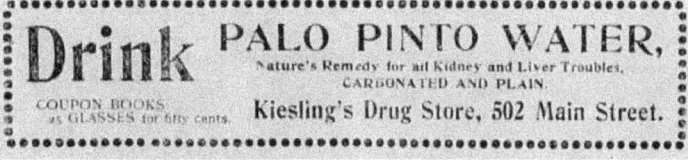

Houston Daily Post, July 26, 1899

502, 504 Main

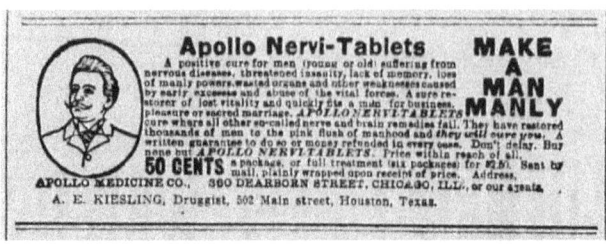

Houston Daily Post, March 16, 1898. Kiesling ad.

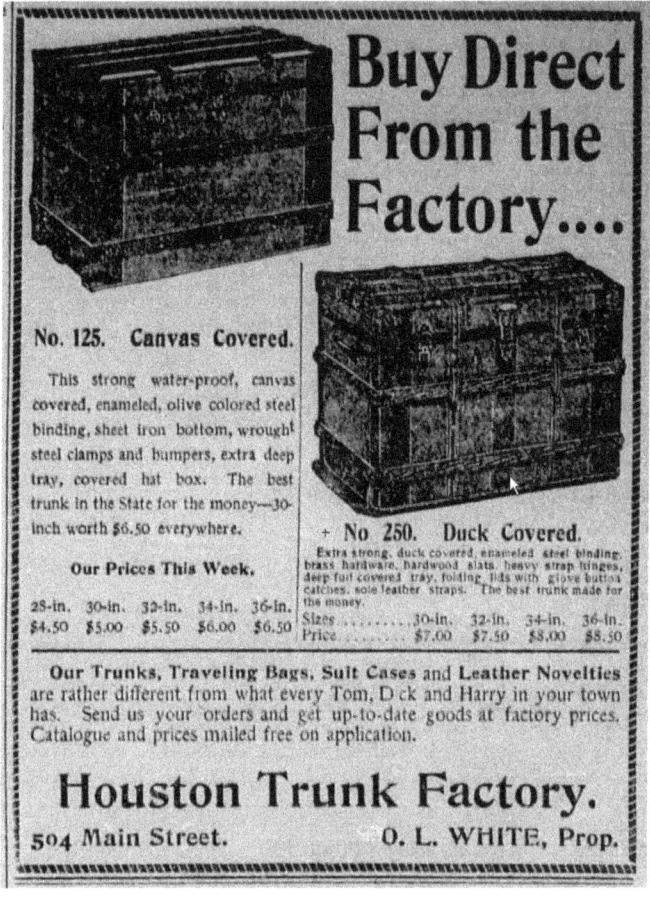

Houston Daily Post, December 3, 1899

Adolph E. Kiesling [9]

Adolph E. Kiesling, druggist, is a native of Houston and a graduate of the Maryland College of Pharmacy, 1889. He entered the drug business in 1881 with E. Erlenmeyer, an eminent chemist. The Kiesling Drug Store in Houston is today recognized as one of the leading drug stores in the state. In point of service and equipment it is not surpassed. Especially is this true of the prescription department, to which Mr. Kiesling devotes most of his time.

Mr. Kiesling represents in Houston the United Drug Company, in which he is a stockholder. It is considered by pharmacists an honour and a privilege to be a member of the United Drug Company, as the members are selected by the organization itself.

---

[9] From *Men Of Affairs Of Houston And Environs: A Newspaper Reference Work.* (1913).

110, 112 Travis
Kirlick Building or Dickson Building

This building was built in 1894 and named for John and Gussie Kirlick. The building was later bought by John F Dickson, founder of Dickson Car Wheel Company, a manufacturer of wheels for railroad cars.

The following is a list of some of the businesses that have been located at these addresses over the years.

Year	Business Name
1908/1909	Vacant, Davidson Bros Wholesale Cigar
1911/1912	Schopmeyer Mfg and Supply Co Hardware, Schopmeyer Mfg and Supply Co Hardware
1919	Lang & Frucht Wholesale Produce, Lang & Frucht Wholesale Produce
1922	Kincaide-Richards Co Fountain Supplies, Kincaide-Richards Co Fountain Supplies
1934	Jamail & Joseph Wholesale Produce, George's Café
1946	Schepp's Wholesale Grocer, Schepp's Wholesale Grocery
1967	Commerce Storage Garage,
1972	Vacant
1976	Huber's Seafood House & Oyster Bar
1984	Huber's Seafood House & Oyster Bar

110, 112 Travis

110, 112 Travis

202 Travis
Cotton Exchange

This beautiful building was built for the Houston Cotton Exchange and Board of Trade. Masons laid the corner stone on June 9, 1884. The Exchange was organized to facilitate the trade of cotton. They moved to a sixteen story building at 1300 Prairie in 1924.

Early view of the Cotton Exchange, circa 1894

202 Travis

214, 216, 218 Travis
W.L. Foley Building

This building was built by John Kennedy after a fire destroyed much of the block in 1860. The building was a Confederate armory during the Civil War. At the end of the war it was looted by Confederate veterans. Another fire destroyed much of the building in 1888, rebuilding resulted in the different heights within the building we see today. The building suffered another fire in 1976 when occupied by The Village Inn Pizza Parlor.

The building is best known as the location of William L. Foley Dry Goods, which occupied the location from 1895 to 1948. William L. Foley was born in Ireland in 1855. He came to America, landing in New York, in 1870. He came to Texas in 1871. His first job was as a clerk in a dry goods store in Brenham. In 1873 he married Miss Mary F Kennedy, daughter of John Kennedy. He established his own dry goods store in 1876. In his first year he had five employees on the payroll. Later he would have 50 to 60 employees. He is known as the "dean of the mercantile industry". Most of the dry goods merchants of the time received all or part of their training in the stores of Mr. Foley.

Mr. Foley sent to Ireland for his nephews, James A. Foley and Pat C. Foley, after the death of their father. It was these brothers who started Foley Brothers, the Foley Department Store that was a fixture of Houston until 2006, when it was absorbed by Macy's Department Stores.

The following is a list of some of the businesses that have been located at these addresses over the years.

Year	Business Name
1880/1881	Harris A. & Bros. Dry Goods
1894	Palace Meat Market
1894/1895	Mcilvain & Dunn "Tenderloin" Restaurant
1908/1909	Foley Wm L Dry Goods
1911/1912	Foley Wm L Dry Goods
1919	Foley Wm L Dry Goods
1922	Foley Wm L Dry Goods
1934	Foley Wm L Dry Goods
1946	Foley Wm L Dry Goods
1955	Vacant
1972	Inn On The Square Restaurant
1976	Vacant
1984	Vacant

214, 216, 218 Travis

218 Travis

214, 216, 218 Travis

214-216 Travis

214, 216, 218 Travis

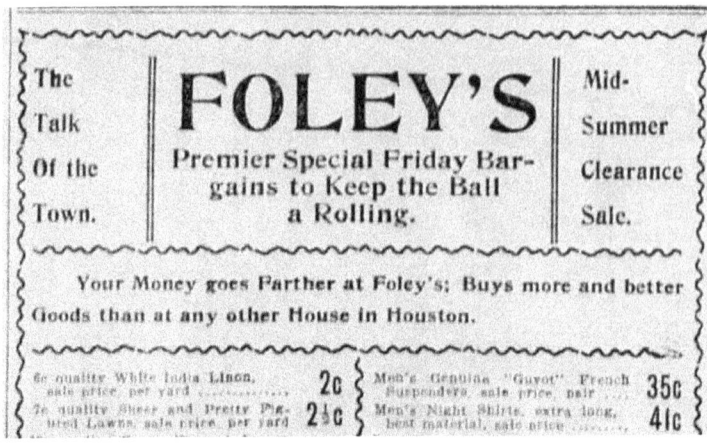

Houston Daily Post, July 7, 1899

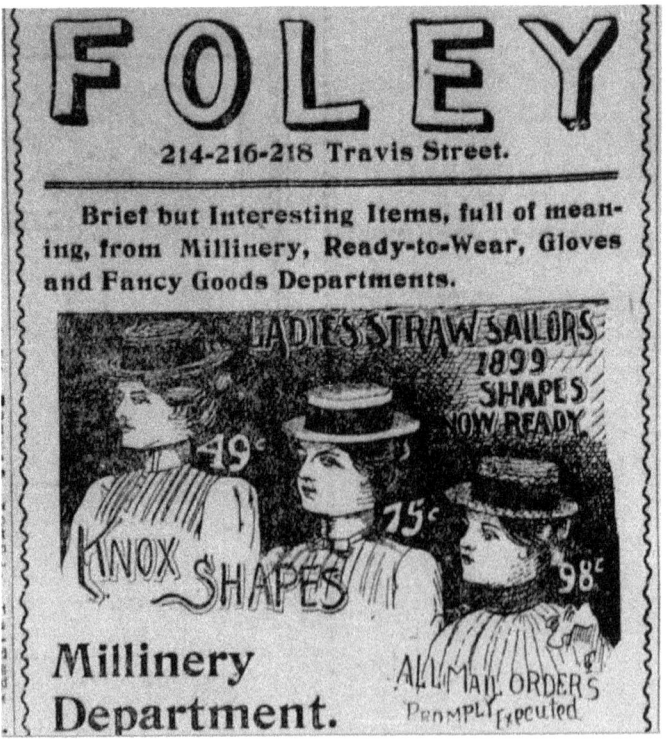

Houston Daily Post, April 21, 1899

214, 216, 218 Travis

Houston Daily Post, December 25, 1901

Houston Daily Post, November 12, 1899

Elegent lady from Foley ad, Circa 1897.

PALACE MEAT MARKET.
H. Edwards, Proprietor. 214 Travis Street.[10]

The trade in meats, fish, poultry, etc., is more than ordinarily well represented in Houston by the Palace Meat Market, conducted under the proprietorship of Mr. H. Edwards, who started his enterprise in 1893, and which has already gained a high place in the estimation of the discriminating public. The premises comprise a three story brick building, 30x100 feet, which is really handsomely appointed and arranged, with every regard to healthfulness and cleanliness. All conveniences are at hand, including improved refrigerators, so that patrons can be expeditiously supplied at the shortest notice, and at all seasons of the year, with the finest quality of beef, pork, mutton, lamb, veal, poultry, game, sweetbreads, fish, oysters, etc. The latter are supplied both in bulk and in shell, the varieties handled being the celebrated Berwick and Corpus Christi oysters. Mr. Edwards caters to the finest trade in the city, and the establishment has already become headquarters for choice supplies in this line, at the same time that the prices will be found altogether fair and reasonable. The proprietor is a gentleman thoroughly understanding the business and all its details. He is originally from Corpus Christi, and has established his enterprise here with the conviction that a really superior market, keeping only the best quality of products, was a necessity to the convenience and comfort of our permanent residents. The success he has deservedly met with has verified the truth of his ideas, and the house is one which is well worthy of patronage and appreciation. Fair and honorable methods of trading are here the invariable rule, coupled to courteous treatment and prompt attention to business.

---

[10] From *The Industrial Advantages Of Houston, Texas, And Environs, Also A Series Of Comprehensive Sketches Of The City's Representative Business Enterprises.* (1894).

305, 307 Travis
Fox-Kuhlman Building

The Fox-Kuhlman Building was built between 1862 and 1866. The widow Mrs. J.C. Fox married John Kuhlman, who owned the property next door. Together they built the current building.

The following is a list of some of the businesses that have been located at these addresses over the years.

Year	Business Name
1880/1881	Levy E. Clothiers & Dry Goods
1894/1895	Doucette, Thomas J. "Lumberman's Club" – Saloon/ Rosenthal, N. Gents Furnishing Goods And Dry Goods
1897	New York Steam Dye Works
1899	A.H. Hess & Co Saddles & Harness
1908/1909	Hess A.H. Harness, Rosenthal M & Co Clothing
1911/1912	Hess A H & Co Harness, Rosenthal Morris Clothing
1919	Jackson O P Seed Co, Famous The Clothing
1922	Jackson Op Seed Co, Famous The Clothing
1934	Jackson Op Seed Co Inc, Famous The Dry Goods
1946	Hollywood Tailors, Reiners Jewelry Co
1955	Hollywood Tailors, Reiner's Loan & Jewelery Co Pawnbrokers
1967	Hollywood Tailors, Galleria Beer
1972	Duke Of Hollywood Tailors, Plaza Madrid Night Club

305, 307 Travis

1976   Duke Of Hollywood Tailors, Plaza Madrid Night Club

1984   Duke Of Hollywood Tailors, Market Square Food & Beverage Restaurant

307 Travis

305, 307 Travis

305 Travis

NEW YORK STEAM DYE WORKS—Ladies' and gents' garments cleaned, dyed, pressed and repaired; agents wanted in every town. Joe Rosenthal, manager, 307 Travis street, Houston; phone 792. 4-17

Houston Daily Post, April 2, 1897

305, 307 Travis

> A. H. Hess & Co., 305 Travis street, saddles and harness.

Houston Daily Post, November 26, 1899

Sidewalk entrance to 305 Travis

JOHN KUHLMAN[11]

About the close of the first quarter of the present century three brothers, John, Henry, and George Kuhlman, emigrated from Germany to the United States, coming probably at different times, and settled in New Orleans. John was a sailor, following seafaring life both before and after coming to America. In his voyage on the gulf he heard a great deal of Texas, and in 1836 visited the country to look it over with a view of settling, provided he was pleased with the prospects. He seems to have been satisfied, for he returned to stay in 1839, locating at Houston, at which place his brothers, Henry and George, subsequently took up their residence, and all three here spent the remainder of their lives. They were all born in Germany, John on December 25, 1812, and Henry and George at intervals of about two years later.

John Kuhlman was a poor man when he came to Houston, and like the industrious, thrifty, German that he was, he accepted whatever kind of work he could get to do, being variously engaged at gardening, farming, saw milling and railroading. As soon as he was able he purchased a small place of his own and settled on it, and from that time on gave his attention chiefly to the pursuits of the farm. He was very saving, and by investing his means in cheap lands and town lots he came, in the course of thirty or forty years, to be a large real-estate holder, and died leaving an estate valued at over $100,000. He was three times married and the head of a numerous household. His first marriage occurred in New Orleans previous to his coming to Texas, and was to Mary Ann Heitman, by whom he had five children, all of whom became grown and three of whom; Mary, Kathrina and Caroline are still living. His last marriage was to Mrs. Sarah Williams, of Houston, a native

---

[11] From *History Of Texas, Together With A Biographical History Of Tarrant And Parker Counties Containing A Concise History Of The State, With Portraits And Biographies Of Prominent Citizens Of The Above Named Counties, And Personal Histories Of Many Of The Early Settlers And Leading Families.* (1895).

of Sabine Parish, Louisiana, born March 9, 1836, and daughter of H. P. and Lavania Stroud, and the issue of this marriage was seven children: Annie Henrietta, Ada, Ida, Henry, George, John, and one that died in infancy. His descendants, children and grandchildren, now number between forty and fifty, and these, with the children and grandchildren, of his brothers, Henry and George, make the Kuhlman family one of the largest of the county. Mr. Kuhlman died in Houston in 1882 and his death was taken notice of by the local press as the passing away of "one of Harris county's early settlers-an honest, industrious, good citizen."

309 Travis
Larendon Building

This building was built by Dr. Joshua Larendon, 1890. Dr. Larendon started the first railroad hospital in Houston, The Houston Infirmary. The doctor had a good sense of humor as evident by the following story.

He met one of his friends on the street, and his friend said, "Doctor you are looking mighty well". The Doctor liked the greeting and decided to use it. A few days later when he met his friend again he said: "The greeting doesn't work. I said that to S—and he replied, 'Gad I am glad to hear that. I was going up to your office for a prescription. I will just save two dollars'".[12]

---

[12] From *The Medicine Man In Texas. (1930)*.

The following is a list of some of the businesses that have been located at this address over the years.

Year	Business Name
1894/1895	Rosenthal Bros. Dry Goods
1898	Fox, I.S. Dry Goods
1908/1909	Fox Issac S Dry Goods
1911/1912	Fox I S & Co Dry Goods
1919	Fox I S Clothing
1922	Fox I S Clothing
1934	Brass Rail Buffet
1946	Rowol Better Tailors
1955	Duke's Man's Shop Clothiers
1967	Duke's Man's Shop Tailors
1972	Aunt Pitty-Pat's Club
1976	Zodiac Distributing Inc.
1984	Facets Cards And Gifts

309 Travis

309 Travis

311 Travis
Alltmont Building

The Alltmont Building was built around 1878. This building was the location of Nathan Alltmont's dry goods store.

The following is a list of some of the businesses that have been located at this address over the years.

Year	Business Name
1880/1881	Alltmont N. Clothiers Dry Goods
1894/1895	Alltmont, Sam Dry Goods And Notions
1896	J A Hall
1897	Beaurecard E Carson Grocer
1908/1909	Mendelsohn Charles Pawnbroker
1911/1912	Mendelsohn Charles Pawnbroker
1919	Uncle Sam's Loan Office
1922	Mendelsohn & Reyemon Jewelers
1934	Karger's Toy Shop
1946	Karger's Toy Store
1955	Karger's Toy Store
1967	Café Hamilton
1972	Vacant
1976	College Inn The
1984	Old Park Grill Short Order Restaurant

311 Travis

311 Travis

311 Travis

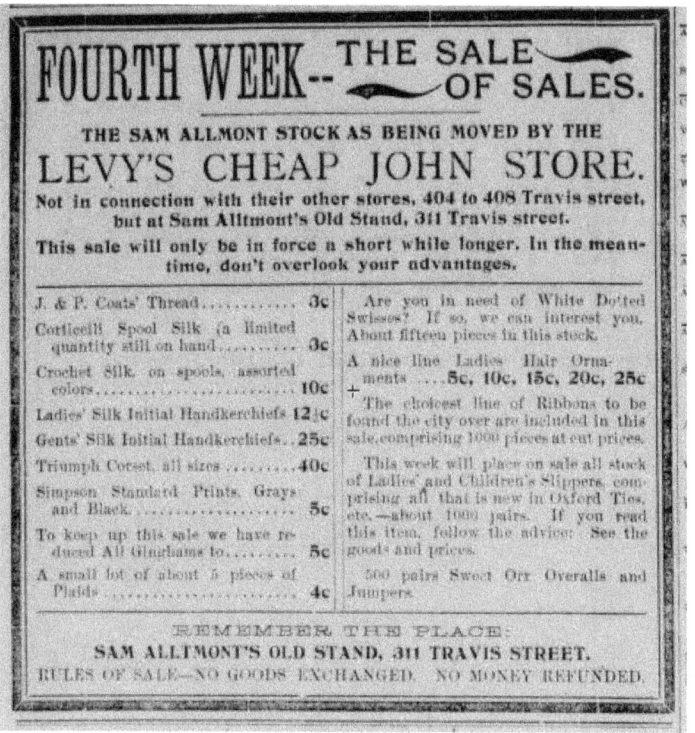

Houston Daily Post, March 1, 1896

Houston Daily Post, October 18, 1896

311 Travis

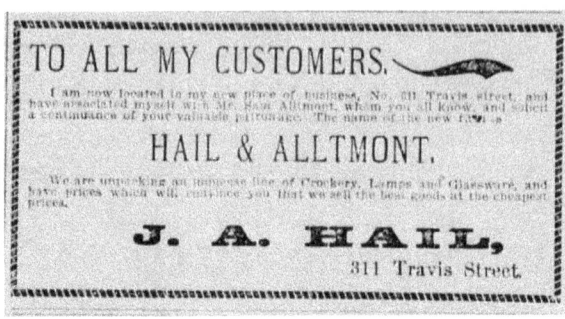

Houston Daily Post, September 27, 1896

NATHAN ALLTMONT[13]

NATHAN ALLTMONT, son of Meyer Alltmont, was born in 1823, in Bavaria, Germany, where he was reared and learned the trade of a merchant tailor. He married Caroline Cramer, of his native place, in 1843, and in 1848 sailed for America. His destination was New Orleans, but the vessel on which he sailed being wrecked off the coast of South Carolina, he made his first landing at Charleston, in that State. He proceeded immediately from that point to New Orleans, where he opened a merchant-tailoring establishment, which he conducted successfully until 1864. This establishment was then succeeded by a general store, which he carried on with still better success until 1872. At that date he came to Texas, and, locating at Houston, 311 Travis Street, here started a general mercantile establishment, with which he was actively connected until his death, December 8, 1893. Mr. Alltmont was a gentleman much respected both in business and social circles in this city, and although at the ripe age of seventy-one years at the time of his decease, his death was much regretted by all who enjoyed the pleasure of his friendship and acquaintance. He was preceded to the grave one week by his estimable wife, her death occurring December 1, 1893. They were the parents of a number of children, most of whom became grown, six marrying. Their eldest born was Alfred now deceased, who left a widow and four children: Nettie, Bertha, Charles, and Alfred. The second child, Jeannette, now Mrs. Max Hart, has two children: Bertha and Meyer. The third child, Jonas, was born in New Orleans, April 15, 1851, graduated at Dolbar's Commercial College at the age of fifteen, was bookkeeper for Levi & Navra for about one year; was a partner with his father from 1884 to 1888; was married July 2, 1884, to Florence Meyer,

---

[13] From *History Of Texas, Together With A Biographical History Of Tarrant And Parker Counties Containing A Concise History Of The State, With Portraits And Biographies Of Prominent Citizens Of The Above Named Counties, And Personal Histories Of Many Of The Early Settlers And Leading Families.* (1895).

daughter of L. H. Meyer, and has two children: Julia and Alfred Meyer. The fourth child, Noah, was born in New Orleans, June 17, 1856; was married November 26, 1882, to Ella Ries, daughter of Solomon Ries, and has one child, Solomon. Noah is manager at the store for his brother Sam. The fifth child, Henrietta, wife of Mose Kahen, has four children: Eugene, Meyer, Alfred, and Sadie. The youngest of the family is Sam, who was born, at New Orleans, March 20, 1863. He received a commercial education, graduating at Euston's Business College, in Houston, Texas, August 6, 1878, at which time he entered his father's store, of which he became manager and remained such till his father's death in 1893, when he succeeded to the business. He was married August 25, 1891, to Miss Florence Sachse, a daughter T. C. Sachse; and has two children: Etta and Nathan.

Mr. Nathan Alltmont, the subject of this brief memoir, was a representative of that large class of German-born American citizens, who, coming to this country without means, and with only an imperfect knowledge of the English language, rise by their own unaided efforts, through industry, economy and correct business methods, from poverty to positions of comparative ease, and who, in so doing, also discharge their full duty as citizens. For a quarter of a century he was in business in New Orleans, and for an almost equal length of time in this city, thus being, in point of actual time spent in business pursuits, one of the oldest merchants in the city at the time of his death. His career here and elsewhere was always marked by the strictest integrity, and by the observance of the most liberal methods of dealing. He assisted public enterprises to the extent of his means, and gave freely to charity. Like all successful merchants, he was chiefly concerned with his business pursuits, but he was social by nature, kind and companionable, and toward his family was a model husband and father. He provided well for those dependent on him, and was, in return, the recipient of the sincerest affection, his children and grandchildren showing now the tenderest regard for his memory.

SAM ALLTMONT,
Dealer in Dry Goods, Shoes, Clothing, Etc.,
311 Travis Street.[14]

The origin of this old established business goes back to the year 1872, when it was founded by the late Nathan Alltmont, the father of the present proprietor. For over twenty years the senior Mr. Alltmont carried on the business alone, until August 1 , 1893, his son, Mr. Sam Alltmont, became a member of the new firm, which was designated N. Alltmont & Son. From 1884 until 1889, Mr. Jonas Allttmont was a member of the firm: Mr. N. Allttmont died December 8, 1893, and the junior member has since continued the business under his own name. His father was a gentleman much respected both in business and social circles in this city, and although of the ripe age of seventy-one at the time of his decease, his death was much regretted by all who enjoyed the pleasure of his friendship and acquaintance. In connection with the business a two-story brick building 25x100 feet in area is occupied. The store is divided into a number of general departments, viz: dry goods, millinery, shoes and clothing, At the head of the millinery department is Miss May Taylor, a lady of fine taste and good judgment; Mr. M. B. Leach is manager of the shoe department, Mr. Theo. Huck of the dress goods department, while as an assistant to Mr. Sam Alltmont in the general conduct of the business, Mr. Noah Alltmont acts as general manager. Each department contains a full stock of goods of the best selection, procured direct from some of the most eminent manufacturers and wholesale dealers in the country. A specialty is made in trimmed hats, and the house has in its employ a skilled trimmer, who goes each season to the various large centers to study the newest fashions of the day, both in imported and domestic novelties, so that

---

[14] From *The Industrial Advantages Of Houston, Texas, And Environs, Also A Series Of Comprehensive Sketches Of The City's Representative Business Enterprises.* (1894).

oftentimes they may be found at this establishment long before they are on view at many contemporary houses. In other departments this concern is equally abreast of the times, and attractive dry goods, shoes, hats, clothing, notions, etc., are here displayed at the disposal of the public at lowest prices. Mr. Sam Alltmont is thoroughly experienced in all relating to his business, of which he has a life long knowledge. For nine years he was its manager before he succeeded to the proprietorship. He is an accomplished buyer, fully understanding the wants of the public in this direction. The business policy of this house is conducted upon that fair dealing and honorable basis which would be expected of a house that has been in successful operation for nearly a quarter of a century.

313, 315, 317 Travis
Baker – Meyer Building

The Baker - Meyer Building was built around 1870. This building was property of Rebecca Baker when she married Joseph F. Meyer Sr.

The following is a list of some of the businesses that have been located at these addresses over the years.

Year	Business Name
1880/1881	Greenwall P.W. Dry Goods/ Roos Simon Dry Goods
1894/1895	Wolf, N. Dry Goods and Notions/ Flaxman F. Mrs. Boots and Shoes
1896	Holtkamp's Hardware Store,
1897	Nathan Wolf Dry Goods
1908/1909	Lang's Oyster Bar, Sauter G F Saloon & Restaurant
1911/1912	Lang's Oyster Parlor, Café Sauter
1919	Cohn & Kaplan Clothing, Cohn & Kaplan Clothing, Miller Isaac Shoes
1922	The Economy Dry Goods, The Economy Dry Goods, Miller Isaac Shoes
1934	Vacant, Economy The Dry Goods, Guarantee Shoe Store
1946	Farmers Seed Co & Hobby Shop, Santa Fe Supply Co No 2, Polmer Tailoring Co
1955	Standard Make Shoes, Rex The Tailor, Polmer Tailoring Co
1967	Le Bon Rat Club, Palmer Tailoring Co

313, 315, 317 Travis

1972	Vacant, Polmer Tailoring Co.
1976	Vacant, Polmer Tailoring Co.
1984	Treebeards Inc Restaurant

313, 315, 317 Travis

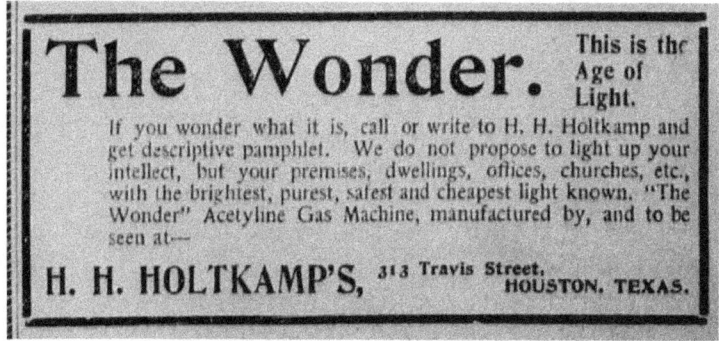

Houston Daily Post, November 19, 1899

313, 315, 317 Travis

Lang's Oyster Parlor, circa 1911.

Houston Daily Post, April 4, 1897

417, 419 Travis
Bolfrass and Roco Buildings

This building looks like one, but is actually two buildings. They were built sometime between 1870 and 1895. The building at 419 Travis was named after Rudolph H. Roco, a grocer. The building at 419 Travis Was named after Christian Bolfrass, a grocer and baker. Both these men ran businesses from their respective address,

David Christian Helberg was a long time tenant of 419 Travis. He came to Houston in 1875, started work in a grocery store, and later opened his own grocery store. He was born March 30, 1855 in Germany. On January 18, 1880 he married Miss Ema Quensell. He died November 1912. According to "The New Encyclopedia of Texas", Mr. Helberg's business was characterized by integrity and fairness.

417, 419 Travis

The following is a list of some of the businesses that have been located at these addresses over the years.

Year	Business Name
1880/1881	Bollfrass C. Bakery/ Bering F.C Grocers
1886/1887	Roco R.H. & Bros. Grocers
1894/1895	Preuss, Emil Bakeries
1899	D.C. Helberg Grocer
1908/1909	Geiselman J.M. Co Meat Market, Heldberg David C. Grocer
1911/1912	Geiselman J.M. Meat Market, Helberg David C. Grocer
1919	Weinstock Bros Grocers, Cohen & Adams Dry Goods Co
1922	Geiselman Gj Meats/Star Cash Stores Number 3 Grocers, Adams & Feigenbaum Co Dry Goods
1934	Kansas City Market No 1/Attra E J Fruits, Adams Ladies Ready To Wear
1946	Kansas City Market Meats/Kansas City Vegetable Market, Adams Women's Clothing
1955	Kansas City Market Meats/Kansas City Vegetable Market, Lane's Inc Women's Clothing
1967	Kansas City Market Meats, Lane's Credit Clothing
1972	Kansas City Market Grocery, Lancer's Club Beer
1976	Cinema Art Theatre, Lanier's Lounge
1984	Vacant, Bubba's Bar-B-Q Restaurant

417, 419 Travis

417, 419 Travis

D. C. Helberg, circa 1911

417, 419 Travis

Houston Daily Post, December 23, 1899

417, 419 Travis

> **When You Read This Item**
> Take it to yourself—consider it addressed to you personally. I have naught but the kindliest feeling for
>
> **Every Groceryman in Houston**
> And would not take a customer away from any, but am aware of the fact that every one at times gets
>
> **Tired and Dissatisfied** and wants to change.
> The first time
>
> **Your Wife Gets That Tired Feeling** Suggest to her to give that fellow HELBERG a trial. We don't want your trade if we can't make it worth your while.
>
> **D. C. Helberg,**
> GROCER,   FINE TEAS A Specialty.
> 419 Travis St., Cor. Prairie Ave.

"When you read this item take it to yourself - consider it addressed to you personally. I have naught but the kindliest feeling for every groceryman in Houston and would not take a customer away from any, but am aware of the fact that every one at times get tired and dissatisfied and wants to change. The first time your wife gets that tired feeling suggest to her to give that fellow HELBERG a trail. We don't want your trade if we can't make it worth your while." Houston Daily Post, December 3, 1899.

CHRISTIAN BOLLFRASS[15]

When a citizen of worth and character has departed this life, it is meet that those who survive him should keep in mind his life work, and should hold up to the knowledge and emulation of the young his virtues and the characteristics which distinguished him and made him worthy the esteem of his neighbors. Therefore, the name of Christian Bollfrass is presented to the readers of this volume as a public-spirited citizen and as a businessman of sound judgment and unimpeachable honesty. He was born in Oldenburg, Germany, November 9, 1847, the youngest of three children born to Herman and Lizzie Bollfrass, who were also natives of Oldenburg, and his sister was Johanna, and his brother Charles Bollfrass.

His youth was spent in the Fatherland, and there, like the great majority of German youths, he received a common-school education and learned a trade; and, while acquiring a knowledge of the baker's business, he also learned lessons of industry and thrift, which were the stepping-stones to his success in later years. In early manhood he decided to seek his fortune in the United States, and soon after his arrival in Houston, which was shortly after he had landed at Galveston, he secured work at his trade, and, by the exercise of close economy, he, in time, managed to acquire sufficient means to enable him to open, in this city, a grocery and baker shop. His excellent goods and straightforward business methods soon brought him a liberal patronage.

Commencing the battle of life, as he did, without a dollar, and dying at the early age of forty-five years, he left the evidence of his industry in an unencumbered estate valued at $30,000, the result of honest toil, judicious

---

[15] From *History Of Texas, Together With A Biographical History Of Tarrant And Parker Counties Containing A Concise History Of The State, With Portraits And Biographies Of Prominent Citizens Of The Above Named Counties, And Personal Histories Of Many Of The Early Settlers And Leading Families.* (1895).

economy, and shrewd, yet always honorable, business management. Socially he was a member of the K. of H., the American Legion of Honor, and, as a citizen, he was liberal in his support of worthy causes. He died December 28, 1891, leaving a widow and one daughter, the latter- Helen- being an accomplished and intelligent young lady. His marriage took place in 1871, and the maiden name of his wife was Louisa Price. She was born in Germany, a daughter of Michael and Louisa Price, the former of whom is still living, at the advanced age of eighty-four years, the latter having died at the age of sixty-seven. Mrs. Bollfrass came to the United States in 1867, and was the second of ten children born to her parents: Pauline, Louisa, Emma. Amelia, Emilie, Matilda, Bertha, Wander, Otto and Emil.

Mr. Bollfrass was a member of the Lutheran Church, as are also his wife and daughter.

910 Prairie
Henry Brashear Building

Built by Henry Brashear, a judge of the district criminal court, in 1882. He built it as an investment property, at the cost of $8,500.00.

The following is a list of some of the businesses that have been located at this address over the years.

Year	Business Name
1908/1909	Gorman & Mcaughan Jewelry
1911/1912	Gorman & Mcaughan Jewelers
1919	Gorman J H Jeweler
1934	Gorman's Jewelry/Burkhalter Jf Gunsmith
1946	Gorman's Jewelry Co
1955	Swift One Hour Dry Cleaners
1967	Swift One Hour Cleaners
1972	Swift One Hour Cleaners
1976	Swift One Hour Cleaners
1984	Swift One Hour Cleaners

910 Prairie

910 Prairie

912 Prairie
Scholibo Building or Shoe Market Building

Built by Charles F. Scholibo, a grocer and baker, in 1880. The first tenant was E.C. Crawford's Texas, Coffee, Tea, and Spice Company. This company was involved in coffee roasting, spice grinding, and was responsible for the "Crawford" and "Fairy" brands of baking powder. "Mr. Crawford was one of the men who saw the coming prosperity of Houston and prophesied it being what it has become, the 'Hub' of Texas and the Southwest".[16]

Si Packard's Troy Laundry was another important tenant.

---

[16] From *The Industrial Advantages Of Houston, Texas, And Environs, Also A Series Of Comprehensive Sketches Of The City's Representative Business Enterprises.* (1894).

912 Prairie

The following is a list of some of the businesses, located at this address, over the years.

Year	Business Name
1885	Texas, Coffee, Tea, and Spice Co.
1894/1895	Si Packard's Troy Steam Laundry
1908/1909	Ineeda Laundry Branch Office
1911/1912	Ineeda Laundry Branch/The Theato Moving Pictures
1919	The Shoe Market
1922	The Shoe Market
1934	The Shoe Market
1946	The Shoe Market
1955	The Shoe Market
1967	The Shoe Market
1972	Vacant
1976	Vacant
1984	Golden Star The Theatre

912 Prairie

912 Prairie

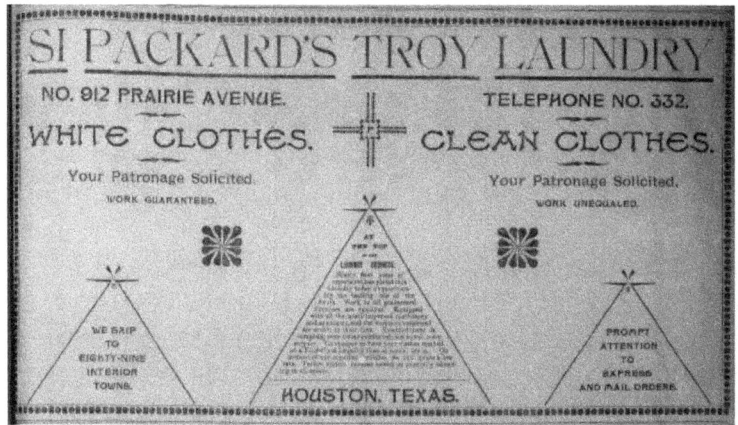

Houston Daily Post, December 17, 1893

Jewish Herald, February 19, 1909

912 Prairie

The Troy Steam Laundry[17]

The Troy Steam Laundry, owned and conducted by Mr. Si Packard, forms the chief enterprise of its kind in the State of Texas. The business was originally founded as Hamilton Bros. & Packard, in the year 1890. On April 1, 1891, Mr. Si Packard became its sole proprietor. The plant may be said to be one of the most complete and well appointed laundry establishments to be found anywhere, It is contained in a two-story brick building, 25x125 feet in dimensions, the whole of which is utilized in the business. The equipment embraces all that has been found useful in modern laundry machinery, which is operated by a 25 horse power engine and a 60 horse power boiler. The establishment is well lighted and all conveniences are available. Among the appliances are a " King " No. 5 collar and cuff ironer, the only one in the State. This machine cost $1600 and it has a capacity for ironing 100,000 pieces weekly. All washers are brass machines-the only ones of the kind in Texas, and the wringers are operated by independent engines. From the inception of the business, the aim of the management has been to do thoroughly first-class work only, and every detail of the business is carefully supervised by the proprietor in person. Every care is also taken that not only shall the work be properly performed, but that no injury shall be done to the delicate fabric and no deleterious chemicals shall be used. Agencies have been established by Mr. Packard in fifty-three towns, and business is obtained altogether from a hundred and seven different localities. The number of these agencies is being regularly increased. The laundry gives employment to forty-one persons, besides a number of teams for delivery. The present capacity of the laundry is 1,000 shirts daily, which number can be increased if required. Upwards of five million pieces are handled annually, and the volume of the

---

[17] From *The Industrial Advantages Of Houston, Texas, And Environs, Also A Series Of Comprehensive Sketches Of The City's Representative Business Enterprises*. (1894).

912 Prairie

transactions is steadily increasing. The sole proprietor, Mr. Si Packard, is a young and enterprising businessman, who believes that what is worth doing at all, is worth doing well. He is a well-known and popular resident, and is a member of the Cotton Exchange, the B. P.,O. Elks, Houston Light Guard, Turn Verein, R. A. R., Knights of Plytias, Post C, T. P. A. and other societies. Si Packard's Troy Steam Laundry is a very valuable part of the general conveniences of Houston, and contributes no little to its comforts and advantages.

914 Prairie
Frederich Stegeman Building

This is another building built by Frederich Stegeman, he also built the building at 502 Main.

The following is a list of some of the businesses that have been located at this address over the years.

Year	Business Name
1908/1909	Turck George V Ice Dealer
1911/1912	Consumers Ice & Oyster Co
1919	Consumers Ice Co
1922	Consumers Ice Co/Farris Jacobs Fruits
1934	Wexler Jas Jeweler
1946	Wexler Jeweler
1955	Wexler J Jeweler
1967	Shamrock Credit Sales General Merchandise
1972	Shamrock Credit Sales General Merchandise
1976	Shamrock Credit Sales General Merchandise
1984	Wig Salon

914 Prairie

914 Prairie

813 Congress
Kennedy Building

This building was built in 1860 by John Kennedy for his steam bakery. During the civil war Kennedy's bakery supplied the Confederate Army with "hard tack", a simple type of cracker or biscuit, made from flour, water, and salt.

This building is said to be the oldest structure in Houston on its original site. The "Shakespeare Coffee House" previously occupied the site, before the Kennedy Building was built.

The building was in the Kennedy family until 1970 when it was sold to William V. Berry, owner of La Carafe, a small beer and wine bar that presently occupies the building.

The following is a list of some of the businesses that have been located at this address over the years.

Year	Business Name
1880/1881	Linder Max Druggists
1886/1887	Ben Levy Druggists
1894/1895	Sewall, L.D. Druggists
1898	Ben Wilbush Druggists
1908/1909	Smith Thomas E Drugs
1911/1912	Wilbush Drug Co.
1919	Wilbush Drug Co.
1922	Wilbush Drug Co /Smith Drug Co
1934	Siegel David Clothier

813 Congress

1946	Gurka's Barber Shop
1955	Vacant
1967	La Carafe Bar
1972	La Carafe Bar
1976	La Carafe Bar

813 Congress

Houston Daily Post

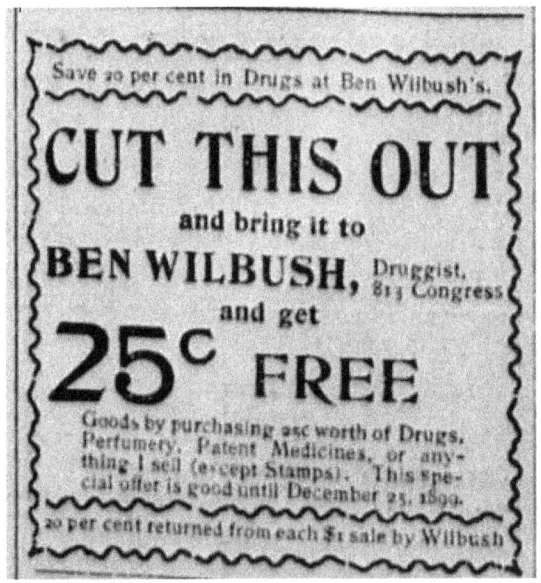

Houston Daily Post, December 23, 1899

> NOTICE—Those who are wearing artificial limbs, and all who are interested in "up-to-date" mechanical surgery are invited to call at my store and inspect an artificial leg constructed by Dr. Bartlett for my sister, who resides at Minsk, Russia. The limb she now wears was made in Germany and weighs eighteen pounds. This one weighs three pounds and fourteen ounces. It is a fact that America leads the world in this branch of artistic mechanism, and I believe that upon inspection you will indorse the statement that Houston leads the U. S. This Yankee product will be started on a journey half way around the world next Monday. Ben Wilbush, druggist, 813 Congress St. 23
>
> PERSONAL—The lady who purchased yesterday at my store 10c worth camphor, for which she paid one coupon, No. 26,407, and one nickel, is hereby informed that said coupon was entitled to $20 in gold. It will be paid her on demand. Ben Wilbush, druggist 813 Congress, Houston.

"PERSONAL - The lady who purchased yesterday at my store 10c worth camphor, for which she paid one coupon. No. 26407, and one nickel, is hereby informed that said coupon was entitled to $20 in gold. It will be paid her on demand. Ben Wilbush, druggist 813 Congress Houston" Houston Daily Post, June 23, 1899

20 Cts. GIVEN AWAY

Cut this out and take it to the druggist named below and you will receive a regular 25c size bottle of Dr. Sawyer's Ukatine for 5c. Ukatine positively cures all forms of kidney difficulties, Dyspepsia, Constipation, Headache, Rheumatism, Puffing of the Eyes. Ukatine cures Pimples and Blotches, and makes sallow and yellow skin white. Do not delay, but take advantage of this great offer, as thousands bear evidence to the wonderful curative powers of Ukatine.

G. W. Heyer, Main and Capitol avenue.
A. E. Kiesling, 502 Main street.
W. D. Hume, Main and Pease avenue.
H. P. Noland, Milam and Preston.
Ben Wilbush, 813 Congress avenue.
A. Seureau, Congress and Chartres.
H. H. Grubbs, 1616 Montgomery avenue.
G. Waples, 907 Preston avenue.
W. B. Washam, 1118 Liberty avenue.
A. R. Ostrander, 2009 Washington street.

Houston Daily Post, May 7, 1899

JOHN KENNEDY[18]

JOHN KENNEDY, the subject of this brief memoir, was a resident of Houston from 1842 to 1878, a period of thirty-six years. He never held any public position of consequence, and never sought to attract public notice. Yet he was one of the most active, and, with a large class of citizens, the most popular, and, in many ways, one of the most useful men that ever figured in the city's history.

Mr. Kennedy was a native of Ireland, born in the village of Tallyoria, county Down, June 12, 1819. His ancestry on his father's side can be traced to Scotland, but by intermarriage there flowed in his veins both English and Irish blood. His people had lived for many generations before his birth on Irish soil, and had become identified in every way with Irish history. His paternal grandfather took part in the revolution of 1798, was seized and imprisoned upon the failure of the patriots' cause, his wife being shot by the hired soldiery of England, and his estate confiscated to the crown. On this account the family was greatly impoverished, and, in consequence, the early years of the subject of this sketch were passed under the most adverse conditions. He received practically no education, but at the age of twelve was apprenticed to the baker's trade in the village of Nuery, from which place he ran away in a short time, on account ill-treatment at the hands of his employer, and went to Liverpool, England. There he resumed work at the baker's trade, and mastered it. At the age of fifteen he left that place and sailed for America, landing at New York. Locating at Hoboken, New Jersey, he went to work at his trade there and made considerable money. He invested this in riverfront property, and thus laid the foundation for what might have been a large fortune had he not met with financial reverses. During the great panic of 1837 he lost

---

[18] From *History Of Texas, Together With A Biographical History Of Tarrant And Parker Counties Containing A Concise History Of The State, With Portraits And Biographies Of Prominent Citizens Of The Above Named Counties, And Personal Histories Of Many Of The Early Settlers And Leading Families.* (1895).

the savings of several years, by the failure of a bank in Hoboken. After this event he came West, and stopping at St. Louis, Missouri, he acquired an interest in a boat and engaged for the next three or four years in trading with the Indians along the Mississippi river. He succeeded well at this, and having heard a great deal of Texas, he decided to try his fortunes in the new country. He arrived at Houston in the fall of 1842, and here opened a small bakery on Franklin Avenue between Main and Fannin streets, in the rear of the present First National Bank building. From this place he shortly afterward moved to Travis Street, near where the Cotton Exchange now stands, and thence to the corner of Travis Street and Congress Avenue, always since known as Kennedy's Corner. Although he made considerable money during his four years' trading among the Indians, most or all of this was lost in an unfortunate business venture with his brother, so that at the date he settled in Houston, he was for the second time since coming to America, a penniless man. His industry, however, and strict business habits soon enabled him to re-establish himself, and in a few years he was again the possessor of some means, with the prospect before him of a successful career. At the opening of the war he owned a steam bakery, a gristmill, and a retail grocery store, all of which were conducted as parts of one establishment, each yielding a good revenue to their owner. In addition to this he owned a large number of Negroes, and had acquired title to several thousand acres of land in Harris and adjoining counties. The Negroes were sold at a sacrifice during the war, and the lands were disposed of as being next to worthless after it became known that slavery would be abolished. Mr. Kennedy held on to his mercantile business, however, and out of this he made some money during the war. He had the contract to furnish the Confederate States government with its "hard tack," and, when occasion offered, he also engaged in the cotton business, running the blockade established by the Federal authorities. After the war he turned his attention more especially to the mercantile business, working into the wholesale trade, at which he met with his usual success. He was engaged in active business pursuits up to the day of his death, and, as the result of his industry, good business management and judicious investments, he left a large estate. But, what was better, he left the record of a life well spent. While he accumulated considerable means, he did not bend his entire energies to the acquisition of wealth. He was willing to live and let live. He knew from observation that many of the inequalities of life are the result of accident, and he was always willing to help, even up, the chances of an honest, deserving fellowman. He invested his means, as they accumulated, in real estate in this city, not to lie unoccupied and be enhanced in value by others improving their holdings around it, but he improved his own, thus furnishing employment for mechanics, as well as adding to the taxable wealth of the city and county. In addition to the business property, which he thus bought and improved, he owned, at the time of his death, no less than sixty houses and lots, residence property which he had thus purchased and improved.

Of plain ways himself, he always lived near the plain people; received from them a liberal patronage, and, in return, was ever solicitous for their prosperity and material welfare. Few men of this city ever possessed more fully the confidence of the people, or used so temperately and for less selfish purposes, the power so possessed. Even the red men of the forest looked upon him as their special friend, great numbers of them always flocking about his place of business in an early day, and giving him a patronage which they refused under all sorts of inducements to extend to others. Old settlers still speak of "Kennedy's Indians," this being the name by which a large band of these aborigines were known, who made Houston their trading place forty to fifty years ago. Mr. Kennedy also lent his assistance to public enterprises, such as in his judgment were calculated to stimulate industry and add to the prosperity of the community. He was a stockholder in numberless undertakings, and contributed much of his time and personal effort to the promotion of whatever measures were calculated to benefit the general public. His contributions to charity were large, and were always made from a sincere desire to do good, and not for self-glorification. Being the only Catholic of means in this city, for a number of years he was the chief support of the church. At his house he entertained the priests and visiting dignitaries. He contributed most of the funds for the erection of the first church building, donated the lots for the present Catholic cemetery, and assisted at all times in taking care of the indigent, infirm and sick of the church.

In 1850 Mr. Kennedy married Miss Matilda C. Thorne, of Galveston, she being a native of Brighton, England, where she was born February 3, 1829, and by this union he had three children: John, Mary F., and Daniel E., all of whom were born at the old homestead, on San Jacinto Street. The daughter was married to William L. Foley, of Houston, and died December 22, 1886. The sons are numbered among the representative businessmen of the city of Houston, both being prosperous, popular gentlemen. John has served as Alderman of Houston six years, is the present representative of Harris County in the State Legislature, receiver of the Houston Belt & Magnolia Park Railway, and a prominent and successful real-estate dealer. Daniel E. is a member of the firm of J. C. Smith & Company, general merchants on Travis Street, and is devoted chiefly to business pursuits. On the 24th day of December 1878, Mr. Kennedy died, followed seven years later, June 21, 1885, by his wife. Both are buried at Houston, where they spent the greater part of their lives, and to which place they were bound, not only by the memory of their early struggles, but by many ties of a social nature.

With the exception of the position of Alderman of the city, Mr. Kennedy never held any public place, but he was a man who always took a lively interest in public matters, and wielded a strong political influence when he chose to exert it.

Wonder is sometimes expressed nowadays that men of such widely different nationalities, and such wholly different tastes, and training as the first settlers of Texas, should have worked together so harmoniously, and successfully, for the up-building of their adopted country, and should have enjoyed so fully each other's confidence, and respect. We oftentimes hear the expression, " One of those old-time fellows, whose word is his bond." The explanation, is to be found in the fact that the men who first settled this country and whose names have survived to us, were men in the true sense of the word. They differed widely in intelligence, in enterprise, in religion, and even in their ideas of government, but in their devotion to humanity, shown by acts of personal generosity, and by the customs of universal hospitality that prevailed throughout the Republic, in their strict compliance with every obligation, whether written or verbal, they were one. In other words, in the essentials of true manhood and good citizenship they agreed. Such was the subject of this brief memoir. In his tombstone appears this inscription, Contributed by one who knew him long and intimately: "A friend to the poor, kind to those in distress, and faithful to every trust."

1016 Congress
Pillot Building

The Pillot Building was built between 1857 and 1868 by Eugene Pillot, businessman and civic leader. The building collapsed in 1988. The building you see today is a replica with the original cast iron columns, sills, and lintels.

The following is a list of some of the businesses that have been located at this address over the years.

Year	Business Name
1894/1895	Davis J.W. Oil Co. – Axel Grease Manuf.
1911/1912	Moore William A Tailor
1919	Packing House Market
1934	Waugh Gene Restaurant
1946	Junior Variety Store
1955	Triangle Loan Service
1967	Rose's Pawnbrokers
1972	Rose's Pawnbrokers
1976	Congress Domino Parlor

1016 Congress

1016 Congress

EUGENE PILLOT[19]

EUGENE PILLOT, one of the old settlers of Harris County, and a resident of Houston since 1868, is a native of France, having been born in the department of Haute Saone, on the 10th day of February, 1820. For many generations, extending back even to the thirteenth century, his ancestors were residents of this portion of France, where they were people of great respectability, mostly farmers by occupation, and manufacturers of oil from hemp and grape seed, and from the seed of the French walnut. His father's full name was Claude Nicholas Pillot, and his mother's maiden name was Jeanne Loiseley. They were born at the close of the last century, the father on August 10, 1793, and the mother on January 3, 1790. They married in their native place, and resided there, where the father was engaged in teaching until 1832, when they emigrated to America, and remained for a time in New York. In the northern portion of that State, and in the city of New York, the father was engaged in the timber business and at his trade as a carpenter and joiner until August, 1837, when he moved with his family to Texas, and took up his residence in Harris County, on Willow creek, twenty-six miles north of Houston. Here he "laid a headright," and established himself as a farmer, following this business with reasonable success until his death, which occurred in the city of New Orleans, in 1863, while in blockade at that places following a business trip to his native country. His wife died three years later, at the old homestead in Harris County. Of their five children, but one is now living, Eugene, the subject of this notice. Their eldest daughter, Hannah, was married to a man named Phipps, and died a number of years later in Harris county, where her descendants now live. The second son, August, (Eugene being the eldest), died in this county in 1844, at the

---

[19] From *History Of Texas, Together With A Biographical History Of Tarrant And Parker Counties Containing A Concise History Of The State, With Portraits And Biographies Of Prominent Citizens Of The Above Named Counties, And Personal Histories Of Many Of The Early Settlers And Leading Families.* (1895).

age of twenty-one, unmarried. The third son, Gabriel, died also in this county, in 1859, leaving one son bearing his name, who lives near Waco, Texas. Rosalie, the youngest daughter, was married to D. Dechaume, and died here in 1864, at the age of twenty-seven, leaving eight children.

Eugene Pillot was just verging on to manhood when his parents came to Texas. On account of the frequent removals which his father found it necessary to make after coming to America, and before permanently establishing himself in this State, the son's education fell short of what it might otherwise have been, but was not wholly neglected, as he had the advantages of some training in the schools of New York State, which was supplemented by private instruction from his father. Young Pillot learned the trade of carpenter and joiner under his father in New York, and put his knowledge to good use after coming to Texas, becoming one of the first builders of Harris County. He recalls the fact that he assisted in putting up some of the first buildings that were erected in Houston, one of which was a small one-story frame structure, which was occupied as a general store and stood on the site of Kiam's present imposing five story brick building, on the corner of Main street and Preston avenue. After a short residence in Houston he moved to the country with his father, and in a measure abandoned his trade, turning his attention to the timber business, which he found very profitable and followed successfully for some time. Later he took up farming, and for twenty-five years was one of the leading planters of Harris County. The rapid settling of the country and increased demand for building material caused him again to embark in the lumber business, which he followed until 1867, at which time he sold out his sawmill interest, and, on January 1, 1868, moved to Houston, where he already owned considerable real estate, to the improvement of which and to other private interests he turned his attention. He is at this writing one of Houston's largest property owners and has also valuable holdings in the city of Galveston. Some idea of the extent of his possessions may be obtained from the statement that his taxes amount annually to between $4,500 and $5,000. His city holdings are what the real estate men call "inside property" and are very valuable, the Tremont Opera House at Galveston belonging to him.

Mr. Pillot has given his entire life to pursuits of a business nature, but has unavoidably been placed in some official positions where his services and experience have been in demand by the public. He has served twice as a member of the Board of Aldermen of Houston, was once Treasurer of Harris County, and is now a member of the Board of Public Works. He was a member of the City Council when the movement was set on foot for the present market house, and as chairman of the building committee it fell to his lot to supervise the erection of that structure, a duty which he performed to the satisfaction of the tax payers of the city and to his own credit. The truth is, Houston has not had, ever among her old citizens, one who has watched her progress with greater interest, or who has lent more substantial aid in that direction than has Mr. Pillot. He has given his active sympathy and support to every public measure calculated to advance the city's interests, while his own personal example of improving his holdings with handsome and substantial structures has not only added to the city's taxable wealth and improved its appearance, but has exercised a wholesome influence by strengthening the confidence of the people in the future of the place and thereby causing others to do the same with their property.

Mr. Pillot has taken but little part in partisan politics, and in fact can hardly be said to be a partisan in political matters at all, since he does not affiliate regularly with any organization. His principle has always been to vote for measures rather than men, but in all contests between individuals, to give his support to the one whom he believed to be the most honest and most capable, regardless of political affiliations.

On January 7, 1845, Mr. Pillot married Miss Zeolie Sellers, a daughter of Achille Sellers, and a native of parish Lafayette, Louisiana. Mrs. Pillot comes of French extraction, and is a member of one of the old French families of Louisiana. She is one of eight children, but two of whom, besides herself, are now living. She has a brother, Peter Sellers, who resides at Hockley, in Harris county, this State, and a sister, Mrs. Amelia Ann House, who lives at Ennis, in Ellis county. Mr. and Mrs. Pillot are the parents of twelve children, six sons and six daughters, only six of whom are now living, three having died in infancy and three in early childhood and youth, Celeste at the age of four, Alexander at the age of thirteen, and Joseph at the age of eighteen. Those living are Julia, now Mrs. Clemille Sellers, of Harris County; Nicholas, who resides near the old homestead in this county; Celestine, the wife of Charles F. Saigling, of Plano, Collin County, this State; Camille, a member of the firm of Henke & Company, wholesale grocers of Houston; Zeolie, wife of Jacob Hornberger, a leading citizen of Houston; and Teoline, clerk in the book and stationery house of W. J. Hancock & Company, of this city. Mr. Pillot has twenty-two grandchildren and four great-grandchildren. Although past the usual age of three score and ten allotted to man, he is still vigorous in mind and body, and continues to give his personal attention to all the details of his business and takes an active interest in all matters of public concern. In the last twenty years he has made no less than seven trips to Europe, spending a considerable portion of the time during his absence in his native country, where he has traveled amidst the scenes of his childhood, and looked up places of interest in connection with the history of his family. While he cherishes that feeling of attachment which it is most natural for one to have towards the place of his nativity, he still regards the country of his adoption as the one to which he owes the strongest allegiance, and of Texas especially he speaks with that peculiar pride and affection which all old Texans are wont to show in referring to the State in which they have so long lived and the making of whose history they have watched from its infancy up.

1402 Congress

This small building was built by Samuel Sam for his grocery business sometime between 1867 and 1873.

The following is a list of some of the businesses that have been located at this address over the years.

Year	Business Name
1873	Sam Sam Dry Goods and Grocery
1880/1881	Mrs. Caroline Sam Groceries and Provisions
1894/1895	Wiener, Jacob H. Druggists
1908/1909	Gomez Sign Co.
1911/1912	Gomez Sign Co
1919	Vacant
1922	Hinchman Auto Supply
1934	Holcomb Auto Supply Co
1946	Bankston Service And Electric
1955	Buster's Record Shop Phono Records
1967	The Old Quarter Beer
1972	Vacant
1976	Old Quarter Restaurant
1984	Vacant

1402 Congress

1402 Congress

SAMUEL SAM[20]

SAMUEL SAM-Pre-eminence is a goal most men strive to attain. No matter in what field, the ambition of the true man will push him to such endeavor that his success will stand out with distinctness. Such is the case with Mr. Samuel Sam, one of the most prominent real-estate men in Houston. Mr. Sam was born in the kingdom of Prussia, now part of Germany, March 14, 1825. He learned the blacksmith trade in his native country and when twenty years of age he determined to seek his fortune in the United States. This was in 1845, and when he reached New York City he had the modest sum of ninety-five cents. Although but a poor boy he was rich in integrity, industry and resolution, and his subsequent career should serve as an example to the young man who, unaided and alone, starts out to combat with life's stern realities. From the city of New York young Sam made his way to Charleston, South Carolina, where an older sister, who had preceded him to this country by a year, was residing, and he entered the blacksmith shop of his brother-in-law, who was then engaged in business at that place. For some time he was engaged in making iron gates and fences, but subsequently business became slack, his brother-in-law suspended, and young Sam was thrown out of employment. Determined to find honest employment of some kind, he went to a boarding house, where he secured work as a dishwasher, for his board. Circulating among the guests he solicited the privilege of cleaning their clothes, blacking their shoes, etc., and accepted whatever they were disposed to give, sometimes receiving five cents, again ten, and in some instances as much as twenty-five cents. Many times it was twelve or one o'clock before he retired for the night, his labors being thus prolonged in the hope of making a few

---

[20] From *History Of Texas, Together With A Biographical History Of Tarrant And Parker Counties Containing A Concise History Of The State, With Portraits And Biographies Of Prominent Citizens Of The Above Named Counties, And Personal Histories Of Many Of The Early Settlers And Leading Families.* (1895).

extra cents. In this manner he saved nine dollars, and with that sum purchased notions, which he started out to peddle, working his way out as far as one hundred miles from Charleston and spending the time from June until September in this work. During this time he saved about $80, and after returning to Charleston he purchased a small stock of fruit and tobacco, and opened a small establishment on the corner of Hallbeck alley and King Street. About this date, 1848, he married, and subsequently opened a boarding house, which he and his wife carried on in connection with the store. Shortly afterward Mr. Sam secured a position on the police force and of course gave almost all of his attention to the duties of that office, his wife looking after the store and boarding house. In this way they made considerable money. Mr. Sam held his position under two administrations, Mayor Snirley and Mayor Hutcheson, and under the latter's regime he was a mounted policeman. In the year 1851 Mr. Sam sold out in Charleston and moved to Clinton, Louisiana, in which city he arrived without a cent. He borrowed $3.75 from Levi Sterne to pay the freight on his household goods; and subsequently borrowed a little more from the same source, with which to buy a peddler's pack. Again he went on the road, and peddled in one parish in Louisiana from 1851 to 1854. From there he came to Texas, and, leaving his wife and children in Galveston, he came to Houston in order to find work. Here he bought a horse and dray and started out in business, following draying but a short time, however, as he found that he was not making very much money. Again he branched out as a peddler and followed this occupation through Austin County until 1857, when, having saved some money, he purchased a store from J. B. Pierce, paying for the same $450. This he carried on for a year and then sold it to William D. Cleveland, father of the present prosperous merchant of that name in Houston. His next move was to purchase a farm in Austin County, and on this farm of ninety acres he opened a store. About the same time he opened two other stores, one at Sempronius and the other at Chapel Hill.

In 1861, when the war broke out, he sold the stores at Sempronius and Chapel Hill, but continued to carry on the other in connection with his farm. Soon after the war opened he began freighting between the agricultural districts of Austin County and Houston, which was then the market place for all the territory northwest of it. He hauled cotton to Houston and goods back, running two ox-teams of five yoke each. He received 70 cents per hundredweight each way, and collected the money on the spot. During the war he also handled livestock and became the owner of a large number of cattle. Shortly after the war he sold his farm and came to Houston. In this place he purchased a lot, on the corner of Austin Street and Congress Avenue, for $2,000 in gold, and later purchased a lot adjoining, for $1,000. On the first lot he built a $5,000 business house, and on the second a tenement house. He also built another small house, and started his daughter in the millinery business. On account of domestic troubles, he turned over all his property to his wife and children, and in 1869 went to work as a roustabout on the "Silver Cloud," a small steamer, plying between Houston and Galveston, receiving for his services $45 per month. From Houston he took a similar position on the "Morgan," and later went to New Orleans, where he embarked on a stern-wheel steamer and worked his way to St. Louis. In that city he worked at different occupations some two years, when, having accumulated a small sum of money, he invested it in a stock of goods and a horse and wagon, and again went on the road as a peddler. He continued this occupation in Missouri about a year, buying rags, feathers and hides, and cleared $1,000. After that he returned to Houston, reaching this city April 20, 1872, and decided to try the dray business again. He bought two mules, three horses and five drays, hired four Negroes, and, taking charge of one dray himself, went to work. This did not prove as remunerative as he had expected, and he sold out, and, in connection with L. Weil, leased a lot of ground on Liberty Avenue, then called the old Liberty road, on which he built a house, and again opened a store. In a few months Mr. Sam purchased Mr. Weil's interest, and conducted the business alone. He was shrewd and possessed of excellent business acumen, and made a great deal of money in this venture. About two years later he leased a lot on the same street, on the J. C. Lord property, built thereon a house 30x60 feet, and carried on business on a much larger scale. This he continued very successfully until 1877, when he sold it to his two sons, Simon L. and Jacob W., and purchased property on the corner of McKee Street and Liberty Avenue, being in business there about two years, part of which time H. O. Gordon was his partner. At the end of two years he sold out this business and turned his attention to Houston real estate. He has been buying and improving, and now owns eighty houses, which he rents, and sixty vacant lots, all of which are in the Fifth ward.

In the year 1848 Mr. Sam married Miss Caroline Sterne, in Charleston, South Carolina, and eight children were born to this union, six of whom survive, Henrietta; Simon L., in the shoe business in Houston; Jacob W. and Levi, in the clothing business in Houston; Joe M., an attorney of Houston; and Sarah. One of his sons, Nathan, died when a young man. May 29, 1890, Mr. Sam married Mrs. Fannie Dryfus, of Houston, and by this union became the step-father of one child, Arthur Charvet. Mr. Sam enjoys the reputation of being a good business man, and is also regarded as a gentleman of the soundest integrity.

1417, 1419 Congress
Askew Drug Building

The Askew Drug Building was built in 1896.

The following is a list of some of the businesses, located at this address, over the years.

Year	Business Name
1908/1909	Jones Randal J W Grocers
1911/1912	Viereck Edmund Druggist, Goodman William T Grocers
1919	Vierick Edmund Drugs, Goodman W T Grocer
1922	Mvdaniel's Drug Store, Goodman L H Grocers / Hruska Edwd Meats
1934	Louis Café, Askew Drug Store No 5
1946	Lee's Coffee Shop, Askew Drug Store #5
1955	Checker Café, Askew Drug Store No 5
1967	Texan Lounge, Askew Drug Store No 5
1972	Texan Lounge, Askew Drug Store No 5
1976	Texan Lounge, Askew Drug Store No 5
1984	H&H Advertising, Askew Drug Store No 5

1417, 1419 Congress

1417, 1419 Congress

2215 Congress

The following is a list of some of the businesses that have been located at this address over the years.

Year	Business Name
1908/1909	Mistretta Joseph Barber
1934	Vacant
1946	Vacant
1972	Houston Coin-Operated Equipment Sales Inc.
1976	Commercial Washer & Dryer Co Industry Equipment
1984	Commercial Washer & Dryer Co

2215 Congress

2215 Congress

> FOR SALE—Good horse and wagon, suitable for light delivery; will sell cheap at once; 2215 Congress.

Houston Daily Post, December 7, 1902. "FOR SALE - Good horse and wagon, suitable for light delivery; will sell cheap at once; 2215 Congress.

1200 Rothwell

Built between 1880 and 1883, was the location for one of Henry Henke's grocery stores.

1200 Rothwell

2403 Milam

Built in 1899, this building is the oldest standing fire station in Houston. The original company was known as Wagon, Steamer and Truck Company, Number 7. In the 1920's the station changed from horse drawn equipment to motorized equipment. The station was in active service until 1968. Today it is a museum for the Houston Fire Department.

2403 Milam

Churches

500 Clay

Antioch Missionary Baptist Church was the first African American Baptist church in Houston, organized by nine former area slaves in 1866. The church was built between 1875 and 1879, with an enlargement in 1890.

500 Clay

1117 Texas

The Christ Church Cathedral an Episcopal church was built in 1893.

1117 Texas

1618 Texas

The cornerstone of the Annunciation Catholic Church was laid in 1869. The steeple was added between 1881 and 1884. The very Rev. Joseph Querat of France initiated the construction.

1618 Texas

Selected Bibliography

Davis, Ellis. The New Encyclopedia Of Texas. Dallas: Texas development bureau, 1925.

Eminent Jews Of America: A Collection Of Biographical Sketches Of Jews Who Have Distinguished Themselves In Commercial, Professional And Religious Endeavor. The American Hebrew Biographical Co., 1918.

Field, William Scott. The Last Of The Past: Houston Architecture, 1847 To 1915: An Inventory And Architectural Stylistic History Of Remaining Early Commercial Buildings. Houston: Greater Houston Preservation Alliance, 1980.

Fox, Stephen. Houston Architectural Guide. Houston: American Institute of Architects, 1990.

History Of Texas, Together With A Biographical History Of Tarrant And Parker Counties Containing A Concise History Of The State, With Portraits And Biographies Of Prominent Citizens Of The Above Named Counties, And Personal Histories Of Many Of The Early Settlers And Leading Families. Chicago: Lewis Publishing Company, 1895.

Houston Architectural Survey. The City of Houston, 1980, 1981.

Houston Daily Post. Various editions, 1893-1901.

The Industrial Advantages Of Houston, Texas, And Environs, Also A Series Of Comprehensive Sketches Of The City's Representative Business Enterprises. Houston: Akehurst Publishing Co., 1894.

The Jewish Herald. Houston: Various Editions, 1911.

Men Of Affairs Of Houston And Environs: A Newspaper Reference Work. Houston: Houston Press Club, 1913.

Men Of Texas: A Collection Of Portraits Of Men Who Deserve To Rank As Typical Representations Of The Best Citizenship, Foremost Activities And Highest Aspirations Of The State Of Texas. Houston: Houston Post, 1903.

Red, George Plunkett, Mrs. The Medicine Man In Texas. Houston: Standard Print. & lithographing Co., 1930

"Texas Historic Sites Atlas," Texas Historical Commission, Austin, http://atlas.thc.state.tx.us.

Various Houston City Directories. Houston Metropolitan Research Center.

Credits

Page 23 Bottom
Houston Metropolitan Research Center
Houston Public Library
Houston, Texas
Houston Photograph Collection
MSS 114-683

Page 31 Top
Houston Metropolitan Research Center
Houston Public Library
Houston, Texas
Business Album of Houston
MSS 145-90

Page 41 Bottom
Houston Metropolitan Research Center
Houston Public Library
Houston, Texas
Business Album of Houston
MSS 145-89

Page 52
Houston Metropolitan Research Center
Houston Public Library
Houston, Texas
HMRC Photo Collection
MSS 114-765

Page 76 Top
Houston Metropolitan Research Center
Houston Public Library
Houston, Texas
HMRC Photo Collection
MSS 114-733

Page 112 Top
Houston Metropolitan Research Center
Houston Public Library
Houston, Texas
Business Album of Houston
MSS 145-146

Page 115 Bottom
Houston Metropolitan Research Center
Houston Public Library
Houston, Texas
Business Album of Houston
MSS 145-20

Houston Daily Post
Library of Congress
Images provided by: University of North Texas, Denton.
http://chroniclingamerica.loc.gov/search/pages/

www.oldtownhouston.com

www.ingramcontent.com/pod-product-compliance
Lightning Source LLC
Chambersburg PA
CBHW031643040426
42453CB00006B/198